As a mother of three sch[...] is the book that will be s[...] on my nightstand to remind me at the end of challenging days that parenting is hard for everyone and to reassure me that I don't have to do anything extraordinary to be exactly what my children need. With all the parenting advice poured out in the world today, it's so easy to feel unequipped, intimidated, and guilty for what we're not doing right. Jeffrey and Amy not only simplify complicated parenting truths into attainable action; they also support these truths with both science and their own relatable parenting stories that make you feel seen and inspired to start again tomorrow. For anyone who's ever felt lonely or unsure in parenting (isn't that all of us?), this book is for you. Thank you, Jeffrey and Amy, for giving us a compass that will always lead us home.

KELLE HAMPTON, author of *Bloom*

I was captivated by this book. While much of it is familiar to me as a clinical child psychologist specializing in attachment, Jeffrey and Amy talk about these truths in a way that make them real and personal. They also link these truths to a spiritual design by a loving God, something very much missing in most faith-based parenting books and curriculums. I will most definitely be recommending it both to my own family and to my clients.

DEBBIE WEBB BLACKBURN, PhD, executive
director of Partners in Parenting

Compared with all the parenting books I've consumed in my decade as a mom, this is the most insightful, encouraging, and relationship-changing one that I've come across. From easy, practical tips to deeper, more thought-provoking passages, I finished this book feeling like I had a new blueprint for how to help my kids thrive. This book was the invitation I was looking for to really nourish my life as a parent.

CLAIRE BIDWELL SMITH, author of *Anxiety*

Amy and Jeffrey's love and respect for parents and children shine through the book and will give light, hope, and encouragement to all parents who long to give their children a healthy and loving foundation in life.

Well-founded in developmental theory and research, their words move us forward to joy in our relationships with our children and God.

WILLIAM F. WHELAN, PsyD, director of the
Virginia Child & Family Attachment Center

This is the parenting handbook I've been waiting for! Marked by wonder, wit, and wisdom, *The 6 Needs of Every Child* offers practical tools for how to parent with love. Each chapter begins with a story that made me laugh, then tear up, recognizing familiar moments with my own children. Just when I asked, "Well, what do I do?" I was handed a new tool. As a mother to a five-year-old and one-year-old, I use the compass in this book every day now. It has already broken old patterns, opened new possibilities, and will accompany our children as they grow. I'm grateful I found this book at the start of my parenting journey! Olrick and Olrick have given parents everywhere an indispensable handbook for our times.

VALARIE KAUR, civil rights activist, author of *See No Stranger*

Wow! This is the one book I will buy and send to my adult kids who are raising kids of their own. And this is the one book I wish I had when I was a new parent. It combines research-based insight with deep moral and spiritual sensitivity, and it is written with both clarity and heart. (I had tears in my eyes more than once in almost every chapter.) Beyond the all-important parenting role, the six-needs framework is helping me better understand myself and others; it is a powerful tool for all human relationships. Where previous generations of parents referred to books by Spock, Dobson, or Chapman, future generations will refer to "Olrick and Olrick" as one of the books that every parent should read. A new parenting classic is born!

BRIAN D. MCLAREN, author of *The Great Spiritual Migration*

Reading *The 6 Needs of Every Child* felt like sitting around my kitchen table laughing and learning with two of my closest friends—one of whom just happens to be a renowned child psychologist. Balancing science and stories, Amy and Jeffrey illustrate that even the best parents make mistakes—and that's completely fine! *The 6 Needs of Every Child* is a practical, relatable guide to establishing a lifelong healthy relationship with your child.

LINDA KAY KLEIN, author of *Pure*

It's so important to have role models of good parenting, and let's be honest, some of us just don't have that. Jeffrey and Amy Olrick speak through the pages of this book like gentle guides, empathetic to the struggles of parents and children alike. It made me breathe a little easier and relax into the best part of being a parent: simply being with my children. Give yourself this gift; you deserve it!

CINDY BRANDT, author of *Parenting Forward*

Full of grace and backed by research, *The 6 Needs of Every Child* was exactly what I needed to recalibrate my parenting with a new focus on connection.

ANNA WHISTON-DONALDSON, *New York Times* bestselling author of *Rare Bird*

Amy and Jeffrey have provided an invaluable guide for connecting with your child. They take the pressure off while sharing helpful approaches to parenting that are grounded in research yet accessible for busy parents.

KRISPIN MAYFIELD, LPC, author, host of the *Attached to the Invisible* podcast

Husband and wife team Amy and Jeffrey Olrick are here to pull back the curtain and shed some much-needed light on how we can all learn to better connect with our kids to parent successfully while also shedding the crippling garb of perfection. From the very first page, this wise, heartfelt, and information-packed book was a balm to my beleaguered mama's soul. Calling all weary parents who are deep in the child-rearing trenches: you'll want to read this one ASAP and definitely with a highlighter handy.

SARAH JIO, journalist, *New York Times* bestselling author

Finally! A book for parents who are ready to break free from obedience-based parenting and move to grace-filled, relationship-based parenting. Amy and Jeff use story and science to seamlessly blend attachment, child development, and faith, clearly leading parents through the six needs of every child. This is more than a "how to do" parenting book; it's a "how to be" parenting book that encourages parents to embrace their unique challenges and strengths, imperfectly sharing the love of God with their children.

NICOLE SCHWARZ, MA, LMFT, parenting
coach at Imperfect Families

AMY ELIZABETH OLRICK
AND JEFFREY OLRICK, PH.D.

THE 6 NEEDS OF EVERY CHILD

EMPOWERING PARENTS AND KIDS THROUGH THE
SCIENCE OF CONNECTION

ZONDERVAN THRIVE

The 6 Needs of Every Child
Copyright © 2020 by Amy Olrick and Jeffrey Olrick

Requests for information should be addressed to:
Zondervan, *3900 Sparks Dr. SE, Grand Rapids, Michigan 49546*

Zondervan titles may be purchased in bulk for educational, business, fundraising, or sales promotional use. For information, please email SpecialMarkets@Zondervan.com.

ISBN 978-0-310-35809-1 (audio)

Library of Congress Cataloging-in-Publication Data

Names: Olrick, Jeffrey, author. | Olrick, Amy Elizabeth, author.
Title: The 6 needs of every child : empowering parents and kids through the science of connection / Jeffrey Olrick, Amy Elizabeth Olrick.
Other titles: Six needs of every child
Description: Grand Rapids : Zondervan, 2020. | Includes bibliographical references. | Summary: "Your child doesn't need a perfect parent, but a present one. Amy and Jeffrey Olrick draw on experience, research, and Jeffrey's work as a child psychologist to help parents discover the power of relational connection. With compassion, faith, and humor, The 6 Needs of Every Child offers insight and tools that will sustain your child for a lifetime"—Provided by publisher.
Identifiers: LCCN 2019052128 (print) | LCCN 2019052129 (ebook) | ISBN 9780310358077 (trade paperback) | ISBN 9780310358084 (ebook)
Subjects: LCSH: Child rearing. | Parenting. | Child rearing—Religious aspects—Christianity. | Parenting—Religious aspects—Christianity.
Classification: LCC HQ769 .O49 2020 (print) | LCC HQ769 (ebook) | DDC 649/.1—dc23
LC record available at https://lccn.loc.gov/2019052128
LC ebook record available at https://lccn.loc.gov/2019052129

Authors are represented by Kathryn Helmers, Creative Trust Literary Group, LLC.

Zondervan Thrive, an imprint of Zondervan, publishes books that empower readers with insightful, expert-driven ideas for a life of thriving in today's world.

Cover design: Micah Kandros
Cover illustration: Juli Hansen / Shutterstock
Interior design: Denise Froehlich
Interior illustrations created with images from: Dan Race/stock.adobe.com, Sentavio/stock.adobe.com, Jan Engel/stock.adobe.com, makc76/stock.adobe.com

Printed in the United States of America

20 21 22 23 /LSC/ 10 9 8 7 6 5 4 3 2 1

To Josh, Drew, and Nathan, of course

Trust yourself. You know more
than you think you do.

—DR. BENJAMIN SPOCK

CONTENTS

INTRODUCTION

It's Hard. This Helps. was one working title we had for this book. *Surprisingly Helpful Information from Imperfect People Raising Imperfect People* could've also worked, though that one seemed a bit wordy. And a title alone can't convey all we want you to feel as you enter into these pages, anyway. So before you begin, will you please pause, close your eyes, and whisper two things to yourself?

I am not perfect, and that is okay.

My child is not perfect, and that is okay too.

Then make room for curiosity by telling shame to move aside.

Being a parent is hard. Most of us have been surprised by both the intensity of our love and by our flashes of anger. We've been deeply disappointed, then ashamed at our disappointment. We've worried more than we thought we would, and we've done things we regret. But there's some good news, news we're about to explore together: we humans grow *through*, not in spite of, hard things. And our imperfect selves are exactly who our imperfect children need to love and care for them.

We started dreaming of this book over fourteen years ago, when our oldest son was two and Jeffrey was transitioning into private practice after working as a child clinical psychologist at The Ainsworth Attachment Clinic at the University of Virginia. Back then we were part of a close-knit church group, meeting weekly with dear friends to share stories and live life together. Most of our friends were also entering the world of parenting, and all of us yearned for a trustworthy road map for that joyful but sometimes harrowing journey.

Jeffrey began compiling tools to share and creating resources that integrated sound knowledge of child development with Christian faith. This, combined with the fact that our first two years of being parents to one child had gone fairly well, made us think we were ready to write. (Everyone, and especially you older parents, please go ahead and laugh at us now.)

That was before we had two more little boys, before the owner of Jeffrey's new practice was embroiled in a sexual scandal, before pastor friends started asking to meet privately with Jeffrey to find out why he opposed gay conversion therapy, before we watched our churches divide and entrench over politics, and before America's deep roots of racism and inequality pushed out from the ground to reveal sinewy vines of hate wrapped around our communities.

Moves and losses and questions about faith and the future crowded in to demand our time and attention. Our youngest son didn't sleep through the night for almost a year, and with three little boys in the house, some days it felt like our walls were shaking with energy. Jeffrey came home from work one evening when the kids were little to find Amy in tears. "What's wrong?" he asked, worried. "Nothing!" she replied. "There is nothing wrong. The boys haven't done anything today but be perfectly normal and active, wonderful little guys. And I'm not sure I'll survive."

At the beginning of our lives as parents, we thought we were ready to write. We weren't. We needed time to let life and parenting break us a bit. We had to spend some years in the trenches, to be tearful in church pews and snappy at our children in checkout lines. We had to walk through shadows that felt like death and to experience God's care for us in ways we never could have imagined before knowing what tools we would keep coming back to and what insights helped hold us together. Some truths have stood the test of time.

We now know that being a parent isn't easy or clean-cut. In fact, sometimes the journey we've been on with our kids has felt quite rough. But that's life. That's humanness. Despite Jeffrey's expert status and our best intentions, we've failed our kids and each other a lot over the years. But failure teaches too. We've found that understanding our kids' wiring—the needs they were designed to have and how we can speak to those needs—helps. It really does. And exploring the intersection of science and our faith has brought life and hope not only to our family but to the many other parents and children Jeffrey has worked with over the past two decades.

Jeffrey's years of work and research have led him to identify six core needs that all parents and kids are born with—delight, support, boundaries, protection, comfort, and equipping. We've discovered it's helpful to have directions to turn to when we feel stuck, so together we've turned these six needs into a compass. With the compass as our guide, we'll use science and stories to explore each need and see how they connect us to growth and to each other. The science empowers us to recognize where our kids are on their journeys and come alongside them as they grow. The stories help explain the kinds of situations the science is speaking to. The misunderstanding, tears, fights, laughter—all of it. Stories of how knowing the essential, inborn needs of our kids allows us to enter into their struggles, and stories of how we can train our eyes to look for what we call "God moments" in the middle of it all.

We hope this book will be a tool for your family, allowing you to see each other fully and love each other deeply. And we also hope you'll be able to enter into these pages without shame or self-criticism, seeing that we have most certainly been in the middle of it too.

We've now had the gift of watching our babies' chubby cheeks thin and narrow into the contours of adolescence. We've listened to our children's dreams, delighted in their talents, and marveled as their legs stretched long and voices changed. We are more convinced than ever that what we do in our homes matters and that the children we're raising matter—to us, to the world, and to God. Time has given us an understanding deep in our bones that we have these children to hold and scaffold for just a little while before releasing them into lives all their own. We can't see into the future, can't control it however much we might want to. So we do our best and offer our hopes and dreams and worries for them up to the God who holds them. The God of the wild and the wilderness, a God who is constantly calling us back to each other and on to love—a love that will not let any one of us go.

Here is what we know now: life can be hard, these tools can help, and love is here to carry us through it all.

BEYOND FORMULAS AND FEARS

How Shall I *Be* with *This* Person?

JEFFREY

Sixteen years ago, on a beautiful, crisp fall day in September, smiling nurses at Charlottesville's Martha Jefferson Hospital checked our baby's vital signs, processed our paperwork, and wheeled Amy and our newborn out the door. I waited at the curb with the car, and as we carefully clicked baby Josh into his professionally-installed-by-the-fire-department car seat, my eyes locked on Amy's. We recognized fear in each other's faces as the magnitude of our responsibility and an understanding of our inexperience hit us in waves. *That was it? They are just going to let us leave with this tiny human?*

I climbed into the driver's seat and wrapped my fingers tightly around the wheel. As I drove, I wondered why I ever thought I could navigate our familiar yet suddenly treacherous streets. Every incoming car felt like a threat, every decision I made had the ability to determine our son's life or death. Amy was perched next to Josh in the back seat of the car, and her mind was spinning as well. *This is just the beginning. What happens next? What are we supposed to do with this baby?*

No matter how our children are delivered to us, the feelings we experience bringing our firstborn home are both uniquely personal and wholly universal. Having children activates some of our most vulnerable, fearful, and wonderful emotions—sometimes all at once. To be human is to seek to understand and master things, and not much feels more important to us than caring for our children well and getting parenting "right." We want to know what to do and how to do it.

And so, even before our children are born, most of us throw ourselves into the act of what we've come to call *parenting*. We read books, go to seminars, and spend sleepless nights worrying that we are getting it all wrong.

But what if I told you that the modern idea of parenting is a fairly recent invention? The concept of parenting spread and gained prominence in the 1970s and '80s as people looked for formulas not only for how to manage their children but also for how to help them grow and succeed.[1] The significance of the term *parenting* has spread since then in response to our particular time and culture, a time when it is rare for people to live in close, multigenerational communities offering help and experience. Parents increasingly worry about their children's financial futures in a culture that places high value on individualism, success, and achievement.[2] In other words, we're told that the stakes are high, we must get parenting "right," and we have to figure out how to do it all on our own.

In generations past, children were raised, not parented. Raising children mainly amounted to keeping them healthy, clothed, and fed as best you could while gradually integrating them into the economic life of the family. This is still the way children are raised in millions of families around the world who live life on the edges of survival. As Western families moved from the edge of economic survival to middle-class security post–World War II, raising children took a more studied bent. Dr. Benjamin Spock instructed millions about the ins and outs of developmental milestones and strategies for soothing teething babies and blistering rashes. And in the last fifty years, a huge industry has sprung up in response to parental anxieties over self-esteem, behavior, achievement, moral formation, and much more. We now have attachment parents, helicopter parents, free-range parents, and achievement-pushing parents. Groups within evangelical Christianity positioned themselves as the standard-bearers and gatekeepers of what they called a "biblical parenting" model for Christians and framed parenting as a spiritual call to arms in the face of a fallen world. Whole curriculums were developed to ensure that children were saved from moral corruption through submission to parental and particularly male authority, allegiance to traditional gender roles, and reliance on Scripture and prayer to overcome "impure" thoughts and feelings that suggested a lack of faith and joy.

Apart from religious expressions of parenting, we've seen a parenting culture develop that often places children's self-esteem and individual achievement above all other considerations. Parenting is sold as a skill to master, and if you do it successfully, you're promised the reward of a baby who can read, a child who doesn't have tantrums, or a high schooler who gets into the college of your dreams. We have been taught to believe that the right tools, applied in the right way at the right times, can get us the outcome we want to achieve—obedient, happy, "saved," successful, emotionally intelligent, mannerly, sleeping-on-a-schedule, safe from danger, realizing their full potential, on-their-way-to-Harvard children. Whatever your metric, there is a parenting program to get you there. With the right formula in place, we can supposedly train our children in *exactly* the way we think they should go.

But what is the right formula? The right way to parent? Thirty years ago experts told us to use star charts and time-outs. Then we found out that star charts had produced a generation of kids without internal motivation because they grew up being rewarded for everything they did.[3] Now we are warned that time-outs may be psychologically damaging.[4] Keeping up with it all is exhausting. You never know which way the pendulum will swing next.

Could it be that all this parenting business is more about our own anxieties and desires rather than the intrinsic needs of our children? And that a particular fixed outcome we have in our minds for our children may have little to do with who they actually are and who they were created to be?

We're convinced it is time to move in another direction. To fully engage in the design and love God has for us and for our children, we must understand and believe something important: human development is primarily a *relational process* that is *constantly unfolding*. Things are and will always be changing, and our children become who they are mostly amid the daily, mundane, and imperfect interactions they have with us over the years. Your relationship with your child is a *journey*, and how you travel together is what matters, not the singular achievements or failures that so easily stand out in our minds to commend or condemn us. The path you're on with your child will stretch ahead past diapers, time-outs, curfews, and graduations and well beyond what you can see today.

Like most modern parents, Amy and I left the hospital with our son wanting to know "What do we *do*?" But our years of parenting and my work as a child psychologist have convinced me that there is a better question to ask. This much better question is "How shall I *be* with *this* person?" Because "What do I do?" is a one-way-street question, and it takes no account of the individual qualities, personality, and needs of the person we are in relationship with. If the answer to our "What do I do?" question is "use time-outs," then that's what we'll do. And it will seem to work, or it won't. If it doesn't, we'll move on to "What do I do now?" until the problem is solved, or we'll give up. Hopefully the problem gets solved, but what happens when it doesn't? Most likely we will feel like a failure, as will our child.

In contrast, "How shall I *be* with *this* person?" is a two-way-street question. It forces us to look not only at our child but at ourselves, and this opens up a whole new world of possibilities. When we explore this question, we learn that any issue we are trying to address with our kid likely has as much to do with us as it does with our child. And the ideas and answers that arise from seriously considering this question will likely lead to an ongoing process of learning and discovery about our child, ourselves, and God. Instead of seeing failure when things don't change, this question invites us to further exploration.

This book explores the idea of being *with* our children rather than parenting *at* them. The six needs we'll share come from a relationship-focused view of parenting and have been described and investigated over the last sixty years through the science of attachment, child development, and neuroscience. We will break open each of these needs from both a scientific perspective and a place of faith, explore what it looks like to meet those needs, and discuss what can get in the way.

If faith is not something you embrace, please do not think you are excluded from what we are about to share. The science presented in this book applies to you and your child whatever your spiritual beliefs. Desiring to understand and meet the genuine needs of our children is a universal human experience—we can recognize in one another the longings, heartbreaks, and love we all have for our kids. So we hope you'll feel comfortable joining with us as we examine the love relationship between children and their parents in the context of our human connectedness. If you come from a different faith background, I encourage you to explore within your own sacred traditions how faith affirms what the science tells us. And if spirituality isn't your thing, we welcome you to be curious or just skip over those sections.

We all do need practical tools to help guide and equip our children as they grow, and I hope you'll find that this book provides much in the way of direction for what to do with your child. But the primary aim of this book is to invite you to reconsider how you approach the idea of parenting. We will explore what it means to be in relationship with your child while navigating a core set of human needs: the needs of **delight**, **support**, **boundaries**, **protection**, **comfort**, and **equipping**.

We've discovered that the six needs of human development come together to form a compass. We want to show you this compass and explain how to use it, believing it can point you and your child toward a scientifically supported and faith-affirming path of purpose and relational wholeness. As you journey together, you'll discover that your path looks different from ours or anyone else's. That's a good thing. Your life and the relationship you have with your child are uniquely your own. We can't know your particular path of purpose and connection; we just want to give you tools for your journey.

Understanding this compass can guide us in our relationships and equip us as parents in life-giving ways, but a compass is not a set of directions. Having a compass to orient ourselves is not the same as typing an address into GPS and selecting a specific route to arrive at a predetermined location. Just as I believe there is no prescribed, right way to be a parent, I believe that you and your family are designed to find your own way together, hopefully in community and relationship with other people who know you and love you and want to see you flourish.

A Long View of the Journey

Learning about the six needs will give you much to think about. You will naturally find yourself wondering not only about how to respond to these needs in your child but also considering how these needs were met or not met in your own life when you were young. You'll become aware of still having these needs and grow in awareness about what shifts need to happen to meet them. We encourage you to be curious. And patient. Change happens gradually.

The good news is that you are already meeting all these needs in your child, in varying measure, and none of the needs have to be met perfectly for your child to thrive. As is true for every parent, it will be more natural for you to meet certain needs than others. There will also be seasons when meeting certain needs is difficult and may even seem impossible. Do not worry. I believe that God made your child to grow toward the light, like a flower in a garden. Your child does not need perfect soil conditions at all times to bloom. Think of these needs as nutrients. Some may be a little low. Some are likely to be just fine. Determine to learn the signs that your son or daughter could use a little more attention to this need or that need and in what situations. Do what you can in that direction. Talk about it with your child. Grow with them.

There may be times that you end up going in circles or feel like you are at the end of the road. Those are the days when the screaming won't stop and no measure of comfort or support is able to quiet the storm or get your kids out the door on time. On days like that, we can feel utterly lost and even scared. Being a parent means being frustrated sometimes and likely disappointed, both in our children and in ourselves. It means having moments of wondering, *How shall I be right now with this person, before I lose my mind and do something I regret?!* and also, *How do I recover from the thing I've already done that I regret?*

Remember that growing a child into an adult is a long and

windy road. As parents, we want to make it easier and less messy. I invite you to stop fearing the mess and the chaos of the moment and embrace a long view of parenting. Believing that parenting is a marathon and not a sprint encourages us to keep going and not to get stuck on the hard days or even the hard years. Accepting that some things may be difficult for a while helps you respond to your child in ways that over time will make things better rather than making them a whole lot worse.

Relationships will always involve moments of incredible joy and connection, as well as moments of pain, rejection, and misunderstanding. Facing those moments of disconnection head-on is a way to strengthen our relationships. Choosing the path of reconnection over and over again teaches our children that healthy relationships are sustained by grace and forgiveness, not by being perfect.

An Invitation to Explore

We hope you'll find this book to be an invitation. It's meant to be a hand outstretched, beckoning you to release some expectations and stop plodding down a path you feel you "should" be on. Expectations can come from any number of places, many of them good—our faith institutions, families of origin, and our own desires to see our kids succeed. But expectations can send us down joyless trails. And when we allow expectations to set the course of our relationships, we take on the role of expectation enforcers and begin to see our children as rebels. Every argument, mistake, unexpected development, faith question, or bad grade risks sending us off course, and so the fear of failure is ever present. Our children's good and innate need to explore and uncover new ground must be constantly redirected. Narrow expectations leave little room for joy or discovery.

But when we choose to stop and breathe and look around, we open ourselves up to the idea that there could be more to see. We discover that our children are born to be explorers and that we are meant to be their companions and guides. Living life with our kids in this way can be a journey of discovery and connection rather than a wearying road of rule enforcement, fear, and disappointment.

Release yourself from the idea of parenting as a job and move toward understanding parenting as a relationship. Learn about our six core relational needs and discover what those needs mean for you *with* your child. And finally, believe that these needs were formed within us so that we can know our children more fully, delight in what we see, and trust ourselves to know how to grow with them every step along the way.

THE SCIENCE OF CONNECTION

AMY

Knowing Where It Hurts: A Story of How Understanding Can Help

Jeffrey and I met during his second year of graduate school, and we've been exploring the needs and concepts of attachment science together ever since. I've learned that when my kids feel safe and things are going well, they naturally move away from me to explore and discover their world. When things get scary or painful, their instincts compel them to draw near me for refuge so they can recover their strength and courage. When Josh was little, he and I were even mother-child test subjects for the Strange Situation experiments Jeffrey's going to tell you about. This influences the way I see the world and interact with our boys.

One summer day several years ago, I was at the pool with a friend when I noticed a young mom sitting in a lawn chair nearby. I noticed her because one of her children, a boy who looked about four, had hurt himself and began to wail. "Ahhh! I have a bleed! Ahhh!! I have a bleed!!" We've all been there.

This brave mama was there at the pool with her little guy and a newborn. She looked completely exhausted, and she kept trying to get her son over his pain by saying things like, "You're fine. There's no blood. Just go back into the pool, and you'll be fine. *Shhh.* You're not bleeding. There is no blood."

I understood her exhaustion and her response, but it escalated the situation. Her son became increasingly agitated, and the more he insisted he was hurt, the more she doubled down. There was no blood, and she could see no bleed. She had no help to offer him as he spiraled into loud and unyielding misery. The situation dragged on and on.

Because I've seen the research and experienced similar situations with our kids, all I could think was, *Oh. He wants to draw near. He's trying to come to you for refuge, and he probably needs comfort. He has a lot going on, too, with a brand-new little sibling, and the physical pain he's feeling is probably bringing everything to the surface. He needs to know you're there for him.* But, of course, all I did was smile encouragingly and sympathetically in the mother's direction because—trust me— it is not a good idea to offer random parenting advice to people you do not know.

Kids usually don't have the sophistication or vocabulary to say what they really mean, so it's best not to get too caught up with their word choices. Bleed or no bleed, this little boy's attachment system was activated, and he did what was instinctual—he tried to go to his mom for refuge and comfort. His little brain wanted to hear her say something like, *Ow, I bet it really hurt when you fell, didn't it? Let's look at it together. Where does it hurt most? Oh, buddy, OUCH. Should I kiss it?*

But in that moment, as is true for me in many of my own moments with my kids, this mom might not have sensed that comfort was what her son needed. Or maybe she just didn't have it in her to provide that comfort. She had needs too, and exhaustion had set in. We all have countless interactions with our kids that don't go as well as they could, and that is normal and human and fine. But ironically, understanding her son's instinct for refuge and turning quickly to offer comfort probably would have helped this mom get her little guy over his pain and back to exploring in the pool much more quickly than denying his hurt. That would have been a relief for her too.

And here's the hard but important part: if that one interaction turned into something consistent—if that mama isn't able to hear or see or speak to her son's need to come to her for comfort, then over time her son will learn that his mom is not a person to go to for refuge. Our four-year-olds may keep trying to return to us, but our twelve-year-olds will have long learned that they need to look elsewhere to manage life's pain—they'll do things like seek reassurance through status and achievement or numbing through screens, drugs, alcohol, and more. I suspect that most of us want our kids to discover how to calm themselves down through us first so that over time they'll be able to steady their own emotions and learn to look for healthy ways to cope with pain.

We're all going to struggle sometimes. That's just the way life goes. The science Jeffrey's about to unpack has helped me understand the hard moments with my kids and navigate through the tough times. It's given me vision to see what my kids need, even when they don't have the words to tell me.

JEFFREY

In 1951 British psychologist John Bowlby proposed something radical concerning human development. Bowlby proposed that love matters. And not just in a philosophical or a poetic sense. Love, he theorized, is our means for survival and foundational to our health and well-being.

The most popular child development theory of that day was called behaviorism, and it put forth a very different view. Behaviorism taught that love and affection caused a child to be needy and dependent. In this way of thinking, love displayed to children was a dangerous indulgence, and proper training mattered most. So Bowlby's report, commissioned by the World Health Organization as a study of the many European children left orphaned after World War II, was groundbreaking.[1] Viewing love as an essential feature of healthy human development was a radical shift and one with profound implications for parenting. Bowlby termed this love—the emotional bond that exists between children and parents—*attachment*.

Bowlby's theory of attachment argued that **all humans are born with two complimentary instincts that shape development: the instinct to draw near to trusted caregivers for safety and comfort under distress and the instinct to go out and explore and master the world around them when the coast is clear.**[2] These two instincts maintain a balance between safety and adventure, preservation and growth. He called them the attachment and exploration systems. And these instincts in the child are paired with a parent's natural instincts to monitor and intervene on behalf of their child, as the situation demands. He called this parenting instinct the caregiving system. These instincts bind us to one another for our survival and thriving. They keep us alive when we're little and vulnerable and prepare us to be contributing members of community as we grow and mature.

Your Child's Instincts and How They Connect to You

Our children's instincts for exploration and refuge-seeking show themselves over and over again as they grow. Your child's world will change and expand as she ages, and her healthy development requires her to push against the horizon of what is new and possible while still needing to return to you for protection and comfort when things get scary or uncertain. Over and over she'll go out to explore, then come back to you to recharge and celebrate her accomplishments. Our children repeat this cycle in many different ways as they develop, and as parents we enter this process with them.

For babies, there is so much to explore that is just out of reach, so your child's exploration may look like eyes scanning a room or looking at you expectantly and grunting while craning for a toy. A kindergartener begs to learn how to ride a bike, an eight-year-old pulls out a cookbook and tries to bake something on his own, your middle schooler wants to go to a new friend's house for a sleepover, and a high schooler asks for your keys to the car.

Refuge-seeking behaviors change as our children grow as well. Your baby's wail tells you that he needs you *now*, and the way your toddler clings to your legs at a birthday party signals that she is not quite ready to explore. As that same toddler gets more comfortable at the party, she may venture out from your legs, but if you watch her closely, you'll notice that even as she plays, she'll glance up every so often to make sure you are still there. You are her secure base, the foundation from which she is able to go out and explore.

As our kids get older, it may be harder to read the cues that they're looking to us for security. Your middle schooler may scan the crowd for you at his band concert, and you'll see a smile flit across his face when he finds you in your seat. Knowing you're there gives him the confidence he needs to play his heart out. Sometimes refuge-seeking behavior in our teens looks like an unexpected text in the middle of the day or a side-hug while you're doing the dishes. Other times our older kids may project the message that they don't need us at all. But understanding attachment helps us know that the refuge-seeking needs are still there.

As a parent, you are hardwired to respond to your child's

exploration and refuge-seeking behaviors. When your infant cries, you feed, change, or soothe her. When she points to something, you track her movement, hand her the toy, and smile absurdly back at her when she smiles with delight. When your toddler runs to you when he sees your neighbor's dog, you pick him up and say, "It's okay, buddy. Spunky is a friendly dog. Let me show you how to pet her." You and your child are constantly moving between your child's need for a secure base to retreat to when distressed and a safe haven to move out from in exploration and mastery. Importantly, these instincts remain with us throughout our lives, though our expressions of them grow more complex and nuanced over time.

The Four Patterns of Attachment

While there are many theories about human behavior, what makes attachment theory so notable and important is that it can be reliably observed and studied, thanks to a woman named Dr. Mary Ainsworth. In the 1970s Dr. Ainsworth developed a procedure called the Strange Situation, which measures attachment in infants and clearly describes differences in how children express and manage their needs for security and exploration.[3]

The Strange Situation is a procedure in which a mother or father caregiver and their child are brought into a playroom and videoed through a one-way mirror. At specifically timed intervals, changes to the situation are made to mildly distress the child. First, a friendly stranger enters the room and begins a conversation with the mother. The stranger then attempts to engage the child as well. Three minutes after the stranger enters the room, the mother is cued to leave. Three minutes after that, the mother returns to the room and the stranger leaves. After three more minutes, the mother is cued to leave her child alone in the playroom. Then, after three more minutes, the stranger enters the room, and after another three minutes, the mother returns while the stranger leaves.

Whether or not children act distressed during these interactions, physiological measures such as heart rate and cortisol levels show that the procedure is, in fact, universally stressful. And what occurs between a child and his caregiver under such conditions has come to be understood as the behavioral signature of a child's attachment. Researchers have identified four types, or patterns, of behavior: secure attachment and three types of anxious attachment.[4]

Anxious-avoidant children have trouble signaling their caregiver that they need refuge when they're feeling stressed. These kids act as if there is no stress or danger even though the situation is inherently stressful—their mother has left them alone in a strange room in a foreign building and without any indication of where she is going or when she is coming back. Their cortisol levels tell us that they are in fact stressed, but they don't express it. These kids don't move to be comforted by their caregiver but instead get stuck in exploration mode.

Anxious-ambivalent children have the opposite difficulty. They have no trouble letting their caregiver know that they are distressed, but they have difficulty being soothed and send mixed signals about their readiness to move back into exploration. They get stuck in seeking comfort and don't move to explore.

Anxious-disordered/controlling children are the most impaired. These children are often seen in high-risk populations and especially in situations where there is a history of abuse, neglect, or a significantly impaired caregiver. They typically have serious deficits in their ability to use a caregiver for either exploration or refuge-seeking. Rather than using the caregiver as a "secure base from which to explore," these kids take on the role of the parent in the face of stress or danger.[5]

Securely attached children are able to move smoothly from refuge-seeking to exploring. In a stressful situation like the Strange Situation, they communicate their distress to their caregiver, try to manage their distress while she is gone, and actively seek out comfort and reconnection when she comes back into the room. Soon they are back to exploring again.

Why a Secure Attachment Relationship Matters

Both the procedure Dr. Ainsworth developed and the patterns of attachment behavior she described have been replicated and expanded on in thousands of studies around the world over the last fifty years.[6] They give us confidence that attachment is an observable fact rather than just an interesting theory. And more importantly, decades of attachment-related research has clarified how different patterns of attachment behavior are related to later human development, across the life span. Summarizing fifty-plus years of attachment-related research, we can say that having a secure attachment relationship helps our kids' development in three important ways:

1. It equips them to regulate their emotions.
2. It gives them a sense of who they are and the confidence to try new things.
3. It protects them from major mental and physical health problems later in life.

Regulating Emotions

Secure attachment interactions train our nervous systems to run smoothly.[7] Scientists call this "emotional regulation." As a central or the central person in your child's life, especially in the early years, you are present with her, reacting to things on a daily, hourly, sometimes moment-by-moment basis. Your calming and comforting her in the midst of your interactions is what teaches her to do this on her own.[8] Through you, her nervous system is learning how to work, or regulate, itself. And the ability to tolerate stress and understand and control emotions is a key feature of psychological health later in life.

Children with secure attachment relationships tend to grow into adults who can experience a broad range of emotions without shutting down or becoming overwhelmed. They have healthier relationships with others and are less vulnerable to mental health problems, including depression and anxiety. They are more resilient to life's stressors and are much more likely to flourish in the face of life's twists and turns. On the other hand, children with insecure attachment relationships tend to be less resilient. Children who become adults with chronic difficulty tolerating and managing a broad range of emotions are much more likely to have strained and unsatisfying relationships and are more vulnerable to mental health problems.[9]

Sense of Confidence

Secondly, our attachment interactions work to establish our sense of self. They help determine how we feel about our place in the world and what we believe we can accomplish. All human beings are born with a drive to pursue what is compelling, determine what is possible, and achieve a sense of mastery over their surroundings and circumstances. Scientists call this "individual autonomy."[10] A child's sense of what is compelling, possible, and satisfying gets shaped in both subtle and not-so-subtle ways by parental response and nonresponse within their attachment relationship.[11] Often, without even thinking about it, parents signal to a child whether their curiosity and inherent motivation is a thing to be celebrated and nurtured or a thing to be ashamed of and suppressed. They can help their kids believe they are competent enough to figure things out on their own, or they can teach their kids that they are incompetent by taking over for them or by being highly critical of their efforts.

Children who become adults with a strong sense of autonomy tend to be more successful academically, show greater persistence when tasks become difficult, take greater risks in life, are more likely to be leaders, and have higher life satisfaction. They move comfortably from seeking help and support to working independently as the situation requires. Conversely, children who become adults with a low sense of autonomy are less academically successful, give up more easily, take fewer risks, and have trouble finding motivation for learning. They have greater difficulty working with others and report lower life satisfaction.[12]

Protection from Future Health Problems

Finally, our early attachment experiences can protect us from major mental and physical health problems later in life. When parents are actively present, responsive, and able to protect their child very early in life from extreme emotional arousal, such as what occurs with neglect and abuse, their child's nervous system is able to develop resiliency.[13] But when parents are absent, unresponsive, or emotionally or physically violent, their child adapts to this stressful environment by developing a nervous system highly attuned to and reactive to stress.[14] This is an effective strategy for surviving in the near term, but it makes children more vulnerable to mental and physical health problems when they face additional stress or trauma later.[15] Children with early histories of neglect and abuse are much more likely to have behavioral problems, academic difficulties, and social difficulties. They are also more likely to have diagnosable mental health disorders and medical diseases, to engage in drug and alcohol use and self-harming behaviors, and are more vulnerable to developing PTSD in the face of future trauma.[16]

Simply put, forget parenting formulas—it's *attachment* that matters. Parents who enter the attachment relationship and meet their children's needs consistently (not perfectly!) raise children who are more secure in their intimate relationships and more competent in the world. They raise children who are better able to navigate their thoughts and emotions and who are less likely to get stuck in unhealthy patterns. While healthy attachment is not a guarantee against hardship or a prescription for any certain outcome, children with secure attachments are in a better position to weather difficulty and to step out into an unknown world with confidence and security.

Attachment and the Six Needs

While I was in graduate school at the University of Virginia, I trained under one of Dr. Ainsworth's first students, Dr. Robert Marvin. At the time, Dr. Marvin was involved with a national study in the United Kingdom assessing a large group of at-risk adoptive children and comparing them with low-risk UK-born adoptive children. The at-risk children had been adopted from Romania after its authoritarian government fell in the late 1980s, and most of them came from horrific institutionalized care settings. They'd had very limited human interaction or caregiving, which meant that most of them had highly disrupted attachment experiences. Dr. Marvin invited me to join him in his work and suggested that my dissertation address a relative hole in attachment research: describing how a parent's behaviors are connected to their child's attachment system. The work we did together affirmed that the way parents respond to their children's needs is linked to the security of their adoptive children, even after trauma.[17]

With colleagues at Tulane University and the University of Washington, Dr. Marvin went on to develop one of the first attachment-based intervention programs for at-risk families. The Circle of Security intervention is now used by early childhood specialists around the world.[18] I took a postdoctoral fellowship to join Dr. Marvin and his colleague, Dr. William Whelan, in this work. Working with at-risk, foster, and adoptive families, we interviewed parents about their own earliest attachment relationships, as well as their current relationships with their children. I spent hundreds of hours watching interactions between children and their parents in the Strange Situation, studying body language, facial expressions, and behaviors as the parents and children came together, separated, then reunited again. The information we gathered helped us create individualized programs for family support.

When I moved on to work in private practice, I discovered a

nagging problem. The parents who were coming to see me all wanted to help their kids. They could see that their kids were struggling, and they wanted to do something to fix it. But many of the parents I worked with couldn't seem to get a proper bearing on the situation. They had theories (he's just spoiled, he's stressed, he misses his dad, he needs to learn a lesson, it's just a phase, etc.), but if they came to see me, clearly the solutions for the theories weren't working. In other words, my clients were lost. They needed direction.

Most parents and families I worked with didn't have access to the intensive resources provided through lab-based Strange Situations, but I wanted to give them the same help that the Circle of Security intervention provided to at-risk families. And so I sought to develop language and tools that were both useful to parents in their day-to-day lives and firmly grounded in attachment and child development research.

My first strategy was to get my clients to ask better questions. Instead of asking *"How can I fix this?"* or *"What's wrong with my kid?"* I steered them to ask questions like *"What might my child need?"* and *"What makes that hard for me?"*

I found that the parents who came to me truly did want to understand their children's needs. Their deepest desire, underneath any frustration or anger or fear, was to know and stay connected to their children. So it made sense to translate the research into the language of needs. This is how the six needs were born.

When our children are using us as a safe haven to explore, research shows that they most actively need our **delight**, **support**, and **boundaries**. When we meet these needs successfully, we promote our children's individual autonomy and a healthy sense of self.

When they are using us as a secure base to receive comfort for distress, research shows that they most actively need our **protection**, **comfort**, and **equipping**. When we meet those needs successfully, we increase our children's ability to manage their own emotions and promote resiliency in the face of future emotional pain and suffering.

The six needs come together to form a compass—a tool you can use on your own journey with your child, to uncover a path forward together, *with* each other.

The Compass of Needs

You are on a journey with your child into an unknowable future, learning and growing as you go. Sometimes the way is clear and easy, and sometimes you feel as if you'll be lost forever. In any case, it is helpful to have a compass: a way to make sense of where you are and where you might turn if you're feeling stuck.

Take a moment to study the graphic below, and then we'll begin to explore how the science of attachment and human development is built into its design.

This relational compass is meant to be a tool for you to use as you journey with your child—a way of discerning your options when you are stuck or a way to know where you and your child are if you want to be more intentional about your path forward.

We'll share detailed descriptions of each of the needs and give you tools to meet them in later chapters. For now, here are some shortcuts to think about and use to remember the needs:

*Three needs make up the "Explore," or
exploration, side of the compass:*

Delight: I see you! Discovering and expressing your love.

Support: How can I help? Anticipating opportunities and obstacles.

Boundaries: How far is too far? Defining and valuing limits.

*Three needs make up the "Draw Near," or
refuge-seeking, side of the compass:*

Protection: Are you safe? Resolving to protect from true harm.

Comfort: I see your suffering. Moving close to ease the pain.

Equipping: Where to from here? Finding a way forward with hope and a plan.

As our children develop, they'll need different things from us at different times, depending on what they're experiencing. To move out into the world in healthy exploration, they need our **delight, support,** and **boundaries**. To come back to us for healthy refuge when things get hard, they need our **protection, comfort,** and **equipping**. As you become aware of these shifts, you'll notice that they happen frequently and seamlessly and that we parents shift how we approach our children depending on the needs they're displaying too.

For delight and comfort, our children need us to slow down and listen. These needs call us to truly see our kids as they are in the moment, whether in joy or in pain, and then reflect that truth back to them. When we are successful at this, our faces and our words give our children an accurate, love-filled representation of who they are and what they're experiencing, like a mirror. For this reason, we call delight and comfort **Mirroring** needs.

For support and equipping, our children need us to draw along-side them and help them evaluate life's practical challenges and emotional storms so they can find their way forward. Rather than simply taking over, doing things ourselves, or fixing things for our kids or, conversely, abandoning them to figure out challenges on their own, these needs call us to act as wise guides. For this reason, we call support and equipping **Guidance** needs.

For boundaries and protection, our children need us to step in and take charge in situations they don't yet fully understand. We step in for our children not to shame or frustrate them but to act as a buffer while their brains gradually grow in capacity to anticipate the consequences of their actions and protect themselves from potential danger. For this reason, we call boundaries and protection **Taking Charge** needs.

Most people tend to lean in the same direction within each pair of needs, and the needs we gravitate to can point us to different well-known parenting styles. We'll list how some of the needs pair with parenting styles in appendix A, but first we want to focus on understanding each need on its own.

The great news is that you don't need to be perfect at meet-ing all the needs to have a securely attached kid. You just need to understand enough about the needs to be able to do an average job of meeting them. Our goal is balance, flexibility, and connection, never perfection.

Your child will not always move in a circle around the compass smoothly and predictably from one need to the next. No, your child will often have needs in many directions, sometimes seemingly at once. So the compass is a tool to help you understand what's going on and to help you find a way forward together when things seem confusing and frustrating.

Now take a minute to look at the compass pointer, both in the graphic above and in the illustration below. Do you see how the pointer has two halves, one representing you and one representing your child? Because of attachment, you and your child are bound to each other and intrinsically connected. You can feel the force of each other—the discomfort of disconnection or the power of connection—even if you don't understand it. And your halves don't always line up. In fact, they often don't. Because there are at least two people involved in figuring out what need your child has—you and your kid—your compass may spend a lot of time looking like this:

In this case, your child's insides are telling him that what he most needs is comfort, but you are sure that what he most needs is boundaries. Who is right? That's something you're going to have to work out together.

When you're misaligned like this, it's not always obvious what your kid needs, and they usually don't know enough to tell you clearly. But if you know your kid and know enough about the needs, then you can picture the compass and take a guess. That guess might look like you trying to comfort your child and seeing if that helps them regroup enough to start moving forward again. Or it could be that you first set boundaries and see where that leads. If you think that both needs are necessary to get you moving forward again, you as a parent will have to take charge of prioritizing and balancing them.

The reality is that in any human relationship, we can see things only from our own limited perspective. If we are honest, we are always guessing. Most of the time parents guess well enough, and we get where we all need to go for this hour or this day, even if it takes a detour with a tantrum or an outburst (from child or parent!). The compass helps you guess more wisely and recover more quickly if your first guess makes things worse.

Turning with Your Child

If you've spent any time studying parenting in a church setting, you've probably heard a sermon about Proverbs 22:6, a Bible verse that is often translated: "Train up a child in the way he should go, and when he is old he will not depart from it" (NKJV). Many people read that verse to mean there is *one* way your child (and all children) should go, and so you must figure out that one way and push your kid down that particular path. But the original Hebrew of that verse points to something much richer. The Hebrew word used for "way" is *derek*, which is the term of a marksman. A closer translation of the original Scripture reads: Train up a child in his way (*derek*); even when he is old he will not depart from it.[19]

Ancient Hebrew marksmen had to craft their own bows and arrows. Once they'd selected the wood they wanted to use to form their tools, they had to look for the wood's *derek*, or "bend." To make a bow that would point an arrow straight and true, a marksman had to know his particular, unique wood and understand how it curved. Marksmen had to be intimately familiar with their material if they wanted to shape it into something that would fly.

If we want our children to grow into adults who are secure in themselves and in control of their emotions, have an understanding of their capabilities, and have a measure of protection against life's inevitable pain and trauma, then we're going to have to know them. We believe that if we follow their bend and watch where they curve, we can guide them toward paths that are purposeful and true.

A Tool for When You Get Stuck

There is one more thing this compass can offer you. When you use it to understand your interactions with your child, you begin to discover that you both have distinct habits. Certain kids are wired to want to explore all the time, while other kids are made to want to stay close and not take risks. You may start to notice when your child's needle stays stuck on a certain side or need on the compass. The compass helps you consider how to use your relationship to help him take risks and grow and how to open yourself up at times when he might benefit from coming close.

You'll start to notice your own orientation as well. Some of us move to protection in the face of every problem, or we love to delight and but have a harder time with boundaries. We often move in one direction or the other because we are uncomfortable with moving toward other needs. These tendencies may be due to personality, or they may arise out of our own histories of having certain needs unmet or overmet growing up. Some needs are uncomfortable to us because they are unfamiliar or, alternatively, too painfully familiar. Becoming aware of these tendencies in yourself is an invitation to greater healing and wholeness.

The compass helps people see not only what their kids need for healthy development but also how their children's behaviors often point to areas of unmet needs. Healing can come when parents begin to understand how their reactions to their children's behaviors often illuminate certain needs that they still have themselves. As we begin to understand and address our own unmet needs, it not only helps our children but gives *us* a chance to heal and flourish too.

ONE MORE LITTLE NOTE FROM AMY

Did you catch that Jeffrey chose to write an entire dissertation on the effect that parents' caregiving behaviors have on the emotional well-being of their children? We were engaged when he started writing, and that honestly made me—the potential mother of his children—feel pretty insecure. All in all, I wouldn't trade a day of being the partner of a "parenting expert." But if anything we write here helps you at all, I wouldn't mind some props for taking one for the team.

3

THEIR NEEDS, YOUR NEEDS

AMY

Wired Together: His Meltdown, My Meltdown

When our oldest son, Josh, was about four, I took him over to our new friends' house to play. Josh loved every minute of the play-date, and when it was time to go home, he was not ready to leave. Screaming and kicking on the floor, he had a complete meltdown in our friends' foyer. Standing in that unfamiliar doorway, wholly responsible for the flailing, out-of-control child at my feet, I felt my stomach knot into a tight fist and my mind cloud with quick, hard anger.

A feeling of panic began to build within me, but I managed to hold myself together enough to get us out the door. Once we got to the car, I released some of the pressure I was feeling on my boy. Through clenched teeth, I spit out cold words. "That is not how we act when we leave someone's house. If we ever want people to invite us back, we need to show them that we are grateful that they had us and not make scenes. I am not going to take you places if this is how you act when we leave" and on and on. My tone was harsh, and I gripped the steering wheel too tightly as we pulled out of the driveway and started down the road toward home. But even as I spoke, I couldn't make sense of my anger.

I forced myself to stop talking, and after a few minutes, the clenching in me began to loosen. I pulled the car over and looked back at my boy. He looked so tiny, scrunched up in his seat as far away from me as possible, staring back at me with huge sad eyes. The pain in his face stopped me in my tracks. What was wrong with me? Why had I lashed out at him like this over something as ordinary and predictable as a little-boy meltdown? Stricken, I apologized for overreacting and told him that I loved him. We drove the rest of the way home in fractured silence. I felt as broken as the air between us.

We visited with that little friend and his mother a few more times during Josh's last year of preschool. After that the boys moved on to different schools and we did not stay in touch. And yet, when I had left our friends' house that day, I felt and acted as if what that other mother thought of me was more important than my relationship with my son. But Josh is the one I share my life with. Josh is the person I now have the privilege of seeing grow into a young man, and who, I'm happy to report, hasn't had a meltdown in a foyer for years.

I share that story because I think it demonstrates how our own attachment systems and the needs we've been taught to value above others can make themselves known in times of stress. In my home growing up, the need for boundaries was heavily valued. I was taught strict behavioral norms, and I knew how unacceptable and disappointing it was when I did not align myself to a particular code of conduct. I learned that to be loved and accepted, I needed to act a certain way—I needed to be *seen and not heard*.

Jeffrey and I had made a conscious decision not to enforce such strict behavioral codes on our kids, which meant that in situations like the one in that foyer, Josh was not thinking that if he didn't hold himself together he would put himself at risk. But that programming was still deep within me. When Josh's temper tantrum made me feel like we were causing chaos, my internal wiring went crazy. My body reacted as if my own survival was at stake. The experience forced me to face hard things within myself and to make a plan for how I would react in the future when my emotions and my own attachment system threatened to hijack my relationships with my boys.

I had to look backward to learn how to move forward with my kids.

JEFFREY

There is a dance of love and emotional bonding that parents and children have with each other—a connectedness that can show us the way to greater wholeness. We parents are the ones who do the leading, and our steps are formed by our own well-worn attachment patterns. These patterns are deeply embedded within us because we began forming them in infancy and practiced them daily through our childhoods with our parents or primary caregivers. We carry these attachment steps into our relationship with our own children. When the steps in our dance remain unconscious, they are largely handed down from one generation to the next, perhaps with just a few changed moves or shifts along the way. But as we learn about the six needs, we also learn how to change our own dance to better fit with our child's natural, God-given design. This leads us to form richer, more secure relationships with our children as they grow. We not only shape who our children become but are also shaped by them.

That is both the scientific foundation and our hope for this book. But there is another basis for this book, and that is our own personal and spiritual journey.

After graduating from college, one of my best friends and I decided it was time to live out the dream we'd had together since high school. We moved to an old row house in downtown Baltimore, right across from Camden Yards baseball park, and I took a job working at a residential treatment home for children. I worked, went to Orioles games, ate crab cakes, and basically lived the good life. Except the good life couldn't mask the growing anxiety and restlessness that had emerged in me during my senior year of college. I had my first panic attacks, which scared me, but I kept them secret. For me, the risk of being vulnerable didn't outweigh the risk of looking the fool. So I kept my fears inside.

But my fear did lead me somewhere. A new friend invited me to church, and because nothing else seemed to be working, I said yes. This church talked about Jesus like he was a living, present, and caring person—someone who had the power to still seas, external and internal. This made me curious, so I explored what Jesus had to say for myself. I went out and bought a Bible, and when I came across the words "Come to me, all you who are weary and burdened, and I will give you rest,"[1] I knew that was exactly what I needed. My mind, body, and soul wanted rest from an anxiety that nobody else could see. So I took Jesus up on his offer. I said, "Here I am, and here you go. Please give me that rest for my soul, because the good life isn't making the anxiety go away, and I am done fighting it." Unbelievably, that is exactly what happened. I experienced a rest and comfort unlike any I had ever known. Life did not suddenly get easy, but I no longer felt like I was alone.

Soon after my Jesus encounter and the spiritual journey it set me on, I started graduate school. At the same time I was professionally exploring the nature of human relationship, I was privately exploring the nature of spiritual relationship with God, studying my Bible just as intensely as I was studying journal articles. And I found striking similarities in what I was reading. I discovered a God who both suffered and comforted, a God who walked along the path with us. This was a God who sent out but also gathered in, who instructed and directed, not with a harsh rod but with a firm and gentle Spirit. This was a God with a sense of humor. A God who delighted. A God who saw me and could discern my needs. A God who looked awfully like the parents who raised secure children. I wondered if maybe this God I was coming to know, this Creator God, could explain the needs that science showed me existed, but with even more depth and meaning.

In the years since, I have come to believe that coming alongside our kids and meeting their needs in the ways outlined by attachment science resonates deeply with the pursuing love of God seen woven throughout the Bible. The two core instincts of exploration and refuge-seeking described by attachment researchers appear to be biological echoes of our spiritual design.

This echo is almost perfectly captured within Psalm 18 of the Bible. David writes in his psalm,

> In my distress I called to the LORD;
>   I cried to my God for help.
> From his temple he heard my voice;
>   my cry came before him, into his ears. . . .
>
> He reached down from on high and took hold of me;
>   he drew me out of deep waters. . . .
> He brought me out into a spacious place;
>   he rescued me because he delighted in me. (vv. 6, 16, 19)

David cries out to his parent God, and God responds. Then, after experiencing God's protective and comforting love, David shifts focus back to the mastery of his world, saying:

It is God who arms me with strength
and keeps my way secure.
He makes my feet like the feet of a deer;
he causes me to stand on the heights. . . .
You provide a broad path for my feet,
so that my ankles do not give way. (vv. 32–33, 36)

What I find most notable in the Scriptures is the collaborative and intimate nature of our spiritual design. We are not alone. God is not at a distance, too busy to be bothered. Nor is the Spirit bossing us around, making us do everything just so. Instead, God is moving with us as we are guided by a beautiful design. We cry out and the Spirit responds with longing, both to draw us near and to launch us out as our hearts ebb and flow in fear and in wonder.

We are all children, loved by a parenting God. I've found rest in this love, and believe it has much to teach us about what our kids need from us too.

The Power of Our Own Attachment Histories

As a parent, I want to understand the needs that exist as part of my children's naturally occurring attachment to me. As a psychologist, I also know how important it is to understand the reactions and feelings that my kids' needs may trigger in me. Because, just like our children, we too are made for connection. We all have strengths and weaknesses in responding to the world and to one another. And guess where many of those strengths and weaknesses come from? They often come from your own attachment history, or the specific ways your attachment figures responded or did not respond to these core needs in *you*. Your attachment system, shaped in you as a child, affects how you parent your own children now. And so, as we move into defining and exploring the individual needs, much of this book is dedicated to the exploration of two interacting questions: What does my child need in this moment? And what is that like for me?

Encountering Pain on the Journey

Embracing the idea that parenthood is a relational journey may feel uncomfortable sometimes because it will require you to consider how your own history affects how you meet the needs of your child. The information we share in this book may open you up to ways in which your needs were not adequately met when you were growing up or are not being met now. So before we go any further, let's consider what unexpected issues might arise as you read. The first is that whatever might be said about your child and her needs is just as true for you and always has been. This opens up all sorts of possibilities *and* pitfalls.

So much pain in families is intergenerational, handed down not simply through genes but through survival strategies we developed in our own childhood. Becoming aware of unmet needs, present or past, can be exceedingly painful. And it is human nature to resist pain. But try not to. Because awareness is also a gift. Understood and embraced, pain can be an invitation to experience healing and greater wholeness for you and your child.

Pay close attention to what feelings stir within you as you read about the six needs. When you feel your emotions rising, I encourage you to do the following three things:

1. **Be still and practice paying attention.** Acknowledge any pain or discomfort you may feel. Do not run away from it or try to shut it down. Take the risk to sit with it.
2. **Be curious about what makes you uncomfortable.** Emotions are generally complex if you allow yourself to scratch past the surface. Anger and sadness tend to be surface emotions. Be willing to ask what other emotions might exist alongside the obvious emotion. Ask yourself where in your life you have experienced this same emotion. Go as far back as you can in your mind, and be open to seeing things about your life you've never recognized before.

3. **Give voice to your experience by either journaling, praying, or talking with a trusted friend or, if necessary, a professional.** This is how you honor and invite your need for comfort, and it is the beginning of healing. It may also lead to equipping, where you are able to identify changes or actions that need to occur in your life or in your family to live into the wholeness that is possible for you.

What to Do When Meeting Needs Is Too Hard

There is another invitation in this book, one less obvious than the others. This invitation grows out of the pain or frustration that may rise up within you when you find yourself unable or unwilling to meet your child's needs. As much as we all want to understand and give our kids what they need, it is easy to misread the moment. And even if you do understand the need your child has in a given moment, you may find yourself disinclined to meet it. You may resist meeting the need because you see it as frivolous or "not realistic." Or you may accept the value of your child's need in that moment but feel like you do not have the energy or emotional capacity to do what the moment calls for. You may even resent your child for having the need. Whatever the case, the result is likely to be conflict and frustration.

This is how it goes sometimes. You are wired to react and to feel when you see your child in need. Your mind and body will remember what it was like for you as a child when you had a similar need, and this can sometimes be a painful process. There is perhaps no greater shame and frustration than seeing your child's needs and not being able to meet them, on top of being reminded of the pain of your own unmet needs.

When this happens, you may want to give up, to think, *This just isn't for me*, even if you believe that these needs are true and good for your child to have. But to respond emotionally to this material is an invitation to create space for healing. Accept the invitation to discover what your pain has to teach you. Don't give up. Resist embracing feelings of failure. Instead, follow the same three instructions as above. **Pay attention. Be curious. Give voice to what you're feeling.**

Jesus asked, "Which of you, if your son asks for bread, will give him a stone?"[2] The statement suggests that Jesus knows parents want to meet their children's needs and to give their children good things. But sometimes it feels like the cupboards inside us are empty—like we have no bread to give. And the pain of that feeling can be so great that we resort to rocklike solutions when our children have needs we cannot meet. We yell. We guilt. We shame. We shut down. We may even become violent. Our children ask us for bread, and we hurl them a rock. Sometimes in the process we will even tell ourselves we are giving them a loaf, thinking, *It's for their own good* or, *This hurts me more than it hurts them.* But in our spirits, we know what it is. We know what a rock feels like because many of us have been thrown rocks ourselves.

There is another story in the gospels, a story about people who were hungry. A crowd had gathered to hear Jesus, and as the hours passed, the disciples wanted to send everyone away to find food for themselves. But Jesus wanted them to stay with him. He asked the disciples to gather all the food they could, and the disciples brought him five loaves of bread and two fish. Looking at the crowd of thousands, Jesus gave thanks for those meager offerings, broke the loaves, and told the disciples to start handing out the food. The bread and fish multiplied into more than enough to feed the whole crowd.

There is good news in this story for us—news that even when we feel inadequate, we need only to bring what we have, no matter how little, and offer it. With prayer and imperfect action, over time we discover sustaining love that carries our children through. What we have will become enough.

But the news is even better than that. We believe that as we seek to meet our children's needs, we can find healing for ourselves too, as children of the One who is with us and takes delight in us.

Our healing happens through a process, just as our children grow through a process. So as we embark on this journey of discovering the needs together, pay attention if painful memories are stirred up within you or if you are dealing with feelings of shame, anger, or inadequacy. Listen to what these alarms want to tell you. Do you need to allow yourself to grieve, to be angry, and to cry? Or to get still and quiet enough to invite God into your frustration to comfort and equip you?

Trusting Yourself along the Way

I also believe that you are already equipped with a deep knowledge about what your child needs in a given situation—your intuition. If you're willing to listen for it, sometimes this knowledge will spring up within you with an insistence that feels very different from the normal knee-jerk reactions you may have. Other times this knowledge may bubble up slowly over time as you reflect, pray, or consult with trusted friends or professionals.

For Amy and me, an even deeper and more mysterious force has become a trusted and essential tool in knowing when to act, and how, with our children. It is a whisper that emerges in moments of quiet and a resonance that guides us as we seek out and listen to counsel. It is something that typically stirs within us but often does not seem "of ourselves." We have come to know this force as Spirit. Many times, it has only been through stepping back from our parenting and declaring our confoundedness and desperation in prayer that the answers we long for make themselves known.

As with a real compass, we believe that the invisible force of the Spirit has the power to move the needle in the direction it truly needs to go. It can be dispiriting to feel like you are going in circles with your child. To try one direction and then another and feel that nothing works. When you feel stuck, it's wise to take a moment to look away from the compass and breathe. To pray, get quiet and ask for wisdom to know, "Which direction is the way to go?" or "How can my child and I move from this place we keep getting stuck in?"

We believe no one is disqualified from calling out and receiving a reply from that which is beyond the ability of science to explain. You do not need to be a "good" person, properly religious, or the spiritual type. Some would say that if your heart aches for healing and wholeness for you and your child, a prayer has already been lifted. You might be surprised at what you hear if you allow yourself to be quiet long enough to listen.

Giving yourself time to stop and get quiet allows you to remember what you know and, if necessary, to develop a new plan. Make room for wisdom to whisper to you so that you'll know if it's time to backtrack or head in a new direction. Trust that eventually you'll make your way through whatever you're facing. Give yourself grace and permission not to be perfect, and believe that opening yourself up to this journey is meant to be for the good of you and your child *both*.

AMY

Where We Can Go from Here

My experience in that foyer with Josh was so jarring that it compelled me to think through what had caused me to react the way I did. Now when I encounter a high-emotion situation, I try to be curious about where that emotion is coming from. I wonder about the expectation or personal value I hold that triggered the reaction and reflect on what I know to be true. Then I try to come up with strategies for dealing with similar situations in the future. Here's an example of what this looks like:

Expectation or Personal Value:	The boys will not make scenes in front of people.
Where It Comes From:	When I was little, my parents enforced strict behavioral boundaries. If I had made a scene, I could have been harshly punished, and causing scenes still makes me feel at risk. Also, I get embarrassed easily, and I really care what people think of me and my kids.
What I Know to Be True:	Sometimes children make scenes in public places. I am my kids' mother forever and the only one they've got, so how I react to them in chaotic moments is much more important than what other people think of us. And even if some people disapprove of us, I have other safe, loving people in my life who accept me and my children as we are.
Strategies for the Future:	Give the boys support and some boundaries ahead of time to help prepare them for new or difficult situations. When things get hard, stop to breathe and think before reacting to difficult emotions. Make room for grace to help me love my kids the way they need to be loved.

Writing out my thoughts and feelings is useful, and getting quiet and picturing the compass in hard times offers direction as well. The compass helps me identify the needs that my own pointer tends to get stuck on, like boundaries, and invites me to consider other needs if one of my boys is struggling. This gives me options to turn to for reconnection when things feel hard or offtrack. Now that I know that chaotic exits are difficult for me, I work to give my kids support to help navigate their experiences. I've learned to give them a ten-minute warning before it's time to leave a playdate and to tell them ahead of time how I would like things to go, saying things like, "Okay, at around three we're going to say goodbye, and it will be hard to leave, but we will see our friend again at school on Monday. Let's work on not screaming and crying when it's time to go, and remember to say thank you for having us."

I think this is what Jeffrey means when he talks about experiencing deep, painful emotions as invitations rather than failures.

Can you think of any known trigger points for you, times when your emotions threaten how you want to love or care for your child? Where do you think that emotion comes from? What do you know to be true about yourself and your child, and where could you turn to reconnect and get back on track?

4

DELIGHT: I SEE YOU!

Discovering and Expressing Your Love

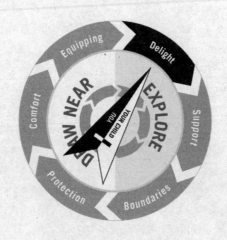

AMY

King's Hawaiian Sweet Bread

Josh was ten when we moved from Virginia to Florida and began attending a small United Methodist Church called Cornerstone. Tucked off the main road and surrounded by community gardens, Cornerstone was pastored by a tattooed, ponytailed man named Roy Terry. Pastor Roy wanted the church to be a place where everyone who entered felt radically welcome, and so he committed to making church gatherings feel like tangible expressions of God's exuberant love. Confetti cannons at Easter, a strawberry festival, potlucks, sending the kids off to Sunday school singing camp songs—if there was a way to make a church reflect the delighting love of God, Roy was all for it.

As we climbed into our minivan after church one Sunday, Josh said, "Church today was fine, but I wish I had gotten a bigger piece of that communion bread. It's good and I'm hungry. The piece I got was *waaay* too little."

At Cornerstone, communion did not come in the form of dry wafers. No, one of Roy's hallmarks was serving King's Hawaiian sweet bread to represent the body of Christ. And the communion servers did vary greatly in the amounts of bread they offered us. Some servers pinched off tiny portions of the loaves to place on our palms, while others ripped off huge chunks to press into our outstretched hands. And King's Hawaiian sweet bread is admittedly delicious, so I understood Josh's disappointment at getting only a small piece. But something about his enthusiasm didn't sit right with me. Almost without thinking, I responded with disapproval. I can't remember exactly what I said, but I'm sure it was something quite earnest about how communion is a time of reflection, to still our hearts and minds and receive God's grace. And if all Josh was thinking about was the taste of the bread, then I wasn't sure he understood what communion was about or even if he should be taking it at all. It's so odd to reflect on it now—how I went into automatic pilot mode, repeating teachings programmed into me since infancy. *Christ's sacrifice is serious, and we must take it seriously. Scheming for more communion bread for the sole reason that you like the taste of it takes the holy out of the sacrament.*

Josh's lighthearted mood vanished, and I settled into my seat to stare out the window as Jeffrey drove us home in silence. Jeffrey had not chimed in to agree or disagree with me, and I honestly wasn't in the mood to hear his thoughts. I grew up in church, and he didn't—he hadn't spent years with this issue like I had. But I felt uneasy about my lecture and hated the feeling of heaviness weighing down the car.

Through the disquiet, something within me pressed up for attention. Not a voice, more like an insistent remembering.

Taste and see.

This was not what I was looking to hear, and I wrestled with the sense I felt rising inside me. *Nope. Not interested, God. I don't want to hear it. I don't feel like being called out right now. I'm trying to teach my kid to honor you, remember?*

The insistence continued—a remembered verse that would not leave me alone. *Taste and see. Taste and see that I am good.*

My life's most profound learning moments have happened like this. An unexpected truth beyond my understanding shows up to correct and clarify my thinking. Love sees that I'm stuck and points me in a different direction. It usually occurs when I'm feeling quite undeniably right.

Taste and see that I Am good. The words wouldn't go away—they demanded attention. I knew I had to consider what they wanted to teach me.

I've read that we all have central lies we tell ourselves about ourselves—lies that return and whisper to us when things get stressful and life feels like too much. For as long as I can remember, the central lie of my life has been *I am a failure.* It's a fear and a belief I come back to over and over again when things are hard. *I am a failure as a friend, as a professional, as a wife*, and perhaps most painfully, *I am a failure as a mother*. Sitting there in our minivan, feeling the tension in the car, I felt invited to examine my lie through the lens of different words, the words *taste and see*. I recalled another communion morning years earlier, a morning that had dawned dark and heavy for me. Our first two boys were little, and a familiar hopelessness had been swirling inside me. I leaned against our kitchen counter and told Jeffrey that I felt like I always let the kids down, all I could see were my mistakes, and that I felt like a completely unlovable failure. Getting us and the kids to church that morning just felt too hard. And even if we went, would we find God there, anyway?

I still remember Jeffrey's reply, how he looked at me from across the kitchen with so much sadness in his eyes. "Oh, honey. I don't believe you're a failure. If you were in a terrible accident today and had to spend the rest of your life immobilized, unable to accomplish a single thing, you would still be wholly and completely loved. I love you and God loves you for *who* you are—what you *do* is not the point. I wish you believed that."

I did not.

Our conversation ended, and we were able to gather ourselves together well enough to get out the door and on to church later that morning. Toward the end of the service, our pastor said that a certain song had been speaking to him that week, so much so that he wanted to play it for us during communion. As the congregation stood and filed toward the front of the church, the darkened sanctuary filled with a plaintive voice singing these lines:

I want your eyes. Be my mirror. Be my mirror. I want your eyes. Tell me who I am. No more lies, no more lies.

Several beats later, another voice joined in, and I listened in silence while waiting to receive the bread and wine. Spoken words cut through the dim sanctuary, saying there was something God wanted me to know: that there was nothing I could do that would make God love me more. And there was nothing I could do that would make God love me less. God loved me because I was me. Nothing could stop that love. I felt as if the words were being whispered straight to my heart.

Beloved, you are my beloved. You are my Beloved. My love comes to set you free from rejection and from shame and from low self-esteem and from despair and from abuse. When I look at you, I see someone I can love outrageously.[1]

I am not making this story up. I still remember the tingling feeling that filled me as I listened to those words—how I pressed a communion wafer to my mouth with trembling hands and lifted the cup from the server's outstretched hand to my needy lips. I felt more heard and seen than I ever had in my life. Would I let myself believe? Would I let myself be loved?

And now here I was, years later, sitting in a car with my son and repeating the same lines to him that God had spent so long undoing in me. Lines that said that there is a right or wrong way to come to God, that we have to perform or shut down our desires or just be a little less like who we actually are if we want God to love us.

Sitting still, riding home from church and remembering, I gasped. Yes, that was it! This is what God had been trying to show me for years—that I am delighted in and free, not because I act unobjectionably or accomplish anything remarkable but simply because I am. My response to Josh had come not from truth or conviction but from a lifetime of self-judgment and religious programming. And even though we were attending Roy's church—a church that offered constant invitations into God's delight—unless I made a conscious choice, I would program those messages into my kids as well.

In the quiet, the Spirit was inviting me to stop and rethink.

A slow smile began to play around the corners of my mouth as

I pictured Josh's disappointment with his altogether-too-little pinch of sweet bread. I imagined God smiling along with me—laughing with delight when Josh said he wanted more bread, that he loved the taste of it and wanted a bigger portion. Isn't that *exactly* what communion is for? To experience how good God is and to be hungry for more?

We were pulling into the driveway now, and I asked Josh to talk to me for a minute before he climbed out of the car. I had some repair to do, and I wanted to look my boy in the eyes, apologize, and give him a hug. I needed to tell him that I had just had a God moment—that I felt like God had spoken to my heart to tell me that my words to him that morning had been wrong. Love had something different to say, something like this:

Come as you are and take the sweet bread—grab a big handful if you need it! Take hold of the cup, pull it to your lips and gulp it down, because God delights in you. Take everything God's offering. God loves you so much—more than you could ever know. Just because you are you. So go ahead and taste—taste and see that I Am good.

And then we would go get some lunch because my boy said he was hungry, and when my son is hungry, it's a joy to be able to give him something to eat.

After that day at Cornerstone, I started calculating the communion lines. Who was serving that day, and who was handing out the biggest portions? That's where I wanted to be. Then, once the server had pressed a big, torn piece of sweet bread into my hand, I did not eat it hurriedly. No, I grabbed hold of it and carried it with me all the way back to my seat, not wanting to miss the chance to savor its sweetness. Once seated, I lifted the bread to my mouth and began to chew, allowing myself to think not only about what it represented but also the real, sweet, and earthy tangible taste of it. Not everyone likes the taste of King's Hawaiian sweet bread as much as Josh and I do, but we both think it tastes delicious. I think God thinks that's a pretty great thing about us. I think it's good.

JEFFREY

Delight: What It Is and Why It Matters

Expressions of delight pop up in all kinds of moments with our kids, and not just in the obvious places. A baby's belly laugh is sure to elicit delight in us. But so can a toddler who has covered herself and the kitchen in a cloud of flour or the teen who has harmlessly fallen backward trying to do a wheelie in the driveway. A parent expressing delight in these moments is experiencing much more than a good laugh at a humorous scene. In times of delight, a deep sense of joy and connection breaks through and spills out—a feeling of *That's my kid! And there is no one else like her!*

Delight lights a person up with wonder and discovery. It is a sudden joy insisting to come out—often quiet but sometimes bursting forth like a trumpet. A genuine experience of delight cannot be faked or forced. On our compass of connection, the journey begins with delight.

Delight often intersects with another important need we all have, the need for physical affection. Especially with our little ones, when we are feeling delight, an urge to wrap our arms around our kids can well up within us, as if somehow we might absorb some portion of their irresistible essence. But while delight and affection might seem interchangeable, they are not. A parent stroking her daughter's hair while they watch a movie together is connecting with her through affection but not delight because you can be affectionate without experiencing delight. Delight requires an attentiveness that affection does not. Delight communicates in subtle, crucial ways—I *see* you. And having seen you, I *enjoy* you. It is in this seeing *and* enjoying with unconditional love and acceptance that delight holds its unique power.

Delight is most often communicated in quiet, small ways. A researcher watching for signs of delight pays close attention to the look of the eyes, the curve of a smile, and the inflection of a parent's voice. An expression so subtle and often so fleeting might seem like it wouldn't matter much. But of all the core needs that we'll talk about in this book, delight is perhaps *the* most important. Researchers have found delight and acceptance to be uniquely correlated to a child's security and well-being. [2] Why would that be?

Think back to your own interactions with your parents. Can you remember a certain look that your mother or father gave you, the sound of your dad's voice or the touch of your mother's hand, and how those things made you feel? From infancy, we humans are designed to study the people around us with a precision and accuracy that no researcher could ever match. Our children are their own scientists, and the people they study most closely are us, their parents.

As a species, our survival through the ages has depended on knowing where we stand with others. You and your child both are exquisitely designed to read faces and interpret what they mean. In fact, our brains have a region called the fusiform gyrus that is dedicated solely to the task of recognizing faces, plus a broad network of regions dedicated to interpreting the meaning behind facial expressions. And of all the facial expressions, the look of delight is the most rewarding, the most comforting, the most empowering. When a child sees a look of delight, they instantly know, *You want me here with you. I am indeed valuable to you, even though I am not adding much tangible value to this relationship and may, in fact, be causing a lot of trouble right now.*

A child seeing and interpreting a look of delight instantly understands that he is safe. Instead of being concerned or confused about his relationship with his parent, a child feeling a parent's delight can focus his attention on discovering what he is capable of and developing his gifts and skills without having to waste energy pleasing his parent or worrying if he is going to be rejected.

But it gets even better. Guess what happens in your brain when you experience delight? Your brain gets flooded with oxytocin, the neurochemical in our brains that makes us feel safe and bonded to someone.[3] Moments of delight between you and your child feel like being in love. And to take things one step further, guess what happens when you get a shot of oxytocin in your brain? Your ability to see into someone's mind increases.[4] This is called *mind-mindedness*.[5] Oxytocin increases our ability to accurately perceive the thoughts and feelings of the person we are feeling "in love" with and see things from their point of view—to hold in our minds the mind of our beloved and not just our own experience.

This means that when you allow yourself to feel delight, you are also allowing yourself to see into your child's world and experience his perspective. This makes you more likely to respond in ways that are sensitive and helpful and thus potentially avoids unnecessary conflict. Delight both emerges from and is sustained by inhabiting your child's reality through her eyes rather than just your own.

When you communicate delight to your child, even in small ways, your child feels it. Your delight gives her a sense of security in who she is and her relationship with you and the confidence to keep exploring and learning to master her world.

What I Most Want You to Know about Delight

When I ask my clients whether they feel delight from their parents, they often respond by telling me that they believe their parents are proud of them. It's easy to confuse delight with pride, but just like delight and affection, these are two very different experiences. We feel and show delight in our kids because of who they are. We feel and show pride in our kids because of what they've done. With pride, the affection rests on their work. Delight is experienced because of who they are. We delight in our kids not because of anything they have done, but simply because of who they are and that they belong to us. They are ours.

The gospels tell a story of parents bringing their children to Jesus to be blessed. The disciples told these parents to stop—perhaps they didn't want Jesus to be overwhelmed. But Jesus corrected his disciples, telling them, "Let the little children come."[6] While the other adults on the scene clearly saw these children only as a distraction and a nuisance, Jesus saw them as people worth attending to. There is no indication from the accounts that the children had any pressing needs their parents were asking Jesus to address—no record of miracles required or questions posed. So why did Jesus take the time to see them, to touch them, to look the children in the eye and whisper blessings over them? Maybe Jesus simply responded to them with delight, as is his nature.

Zephaniah 3:17 (NIV 1984) reads,

> The LORD your God is with you,
>   he is mighty to save.
> He will take great delight in you,
>   he will quiet you with his love,
>   he will rejoice over you with singing.

In the words of the ancient Hebrew writer, the creator of the universe is with you and seeks to delight in you, to quiet you and *rejoice over you with singing*. Please let that sink in. The possibility that God delights in you is potentially more radical and disruptive than the possibility that God loves you in a general sense.

In the Christian tradition, the type of love most often emphasized is a sacrificial love. But sacrifice does not require delight. Any parent who has gone without sleep to nurse a sick baby, who has worked double shifts to put food on the table, who has sold everything to flee violence and seek safety for their child has done so out of a beautiful and sacrificial love. Many of us have felt the sacrificing love of our own parents and have come to receive that as affirmation of their deep love. God's love is no less sacrificial and determined, but God's love for you is much more than sacrifice. So much more. It is a laughing out loud, singing out loud, dancing over you love. There is nothing you can do to stop it. And this love is not waiting for you to prove yourself worthy of such extravagance. It precedes you and your actions. You were made for this delighting love, and so was your child. We all need this kind of love to thrive and flourish.

At the beginning of his ministry, Jesus went to Galilee to be baptized by John the Baptist. As John lifted Jesus out of the water, the gospels tell us that the Spirit descended on Jesus like a dove, and the voice of God declared, "This is my beloved son, in whom I am well pleased."[7] Various translations include "I take delight in him!" and "He brings me great joy!"

The timing of this declaration of pleasure is extraordinary. Jesus had not yet begun his ministry. He had not yet done all the things he would go on to do that might "earn" this expression of love and delight. He had not healed a single person, set a single religious person straight, or spoken to the multitudes about the mysteries of God. God's extravagant proclamation of love came *before* the temptation, before the miracles, before the teaching, before the cross. The delight preceded the work. Jesus was sent into the world with a clear understanding of God's delight in him. Delight came first.

Was the baptism of Jesus in fact a baptism into God's pleasure, God's delight, God's joy? And might everything that followed have flowed out of that baptism? And if it did, what might that mean for us? For our children?

Science and faith come together to show us the essential role that delight has in our growing into our full potential. Delight builds a foundation for emotional and relational safety, and from that safety, our kids can explore and grow into their God-given talents and abilities. I tell parents that delight is the wind in their children's sails. It provides the lift they need to set them off into the world. Delight doesn't guarantee any concrete outcomes but is a hedge against the storms. If our kids are set off with sails full of delight, they can run aground. They can fail. Your child's knowledge of your delight deep in his bones means that when the storm clears and the ship is righted, he can be audacious enough to hoist the sail again. An inheritance of delight is a wind that stays with our kids long after they are grown.

When Delighting Feels Hard

You may be thinking, *But what if I don't feel delight? Half the time I'm frustrated, irritated, angry, or exhausted. The other half of the time, I'm running around just trying to get through the day. Time for delight feels like a luxury I can't afford. How am I supposed to feel delight then?* Well, me too. But don't give up, because the bar is lower than you think. Delight is so powerful that even small doses can make a huge difference in your child's well-being and developmental trajectory.

There is no way around it: if you are going to meet your child's need for delight, it will cost you some time. But what most people don't realize is that much of the "getting through the day" of parenting—the meltdowns, the negative behavior—is a direct result of a child's diminished sense of parental attention and delight, especially with younger children. My mentor, Dr. Marvin, likened it to a battery. When a child's delight battery gets low, they act up in ways that draw you in, but usually in a negative cycle of attention. But when you proactively recharge that battery, a child's natural tendency to explore independently and display competence kicks in. Taking time to see your child and express delight decreases the likelihood that you'll be spending time with him later fighting battles of obedience or engaging in the sorts of negative interactions that tend to go on and on and sap all your energy.

But what does it mean to "charge the delight battery"? More than anything, it means taking time to attend to your child *without distraction*. Think about how you feel when somebody is looking at their phone while you try to connect with them. It destroys any sense of being a genuine object of affection, no matter how much they smile at you between glances at their screen. You cannot lose yourself in someone if some part of your brain is elsewhere. And at the heart of delight is letting yourself enter into your child's experience.

If we are to press in to this need, we are going to have to give ourselves permission to be still more, even if that means being late, cancelling a meeting, or leaving the dishes for tomorrow. But creating space for delight does not necessarily mean setting aside huge amounts of time. Our children bombard us with little solicitations for delight all the time. The pictures they show you, the stories they want to tell, the "look at me" moments that even your teenagers still angle for. Grab these little opportunities when they come. Let yourself pause, look, and declare, "I see you! And I love *who* I see!" Quiet yourself and discover delight hiding in plain sight. Ask yourself the question, "Who is this child God has given me?" Inhabit your child's perspective for a moment rather than rushing in with your own view of things. Let yourself just observe with curiosity and wonder.

Sometimes it's more than busyness and the siren distraction of digital devices that rob us of delight for our children. Sometimes our own emotional lives suffocate delight before it can see the light of day. The reality is that our children's presence often means that there is a something we have to do—a demand, a danger, or just an inconvenience we have to respond to. An endless train of need can put parents in the mental and emotional position of "What do I have to do now?" This is a setup for irritability, frustration, anger, fear, and all sorts of other powerful emotions.

To overcome the emotions that get in the way of delight, we must first simply acknowledge them. Saying "I am tired" is an act of self-awareness and compassion, because a feeling is what it is. Feeling something is always valid—problems only arise when we behave poorly in reaction to our feelings.

The ability to name a feeling is a skill that all of us need to have and many of us have yet to acquire. Don't worry, you're never too old to learn! We are going to learn more about how to do it in the chapter about comfort, but for now try to settle in with the idea that naming a feeling is a big empowering deal all by itself. Naming a negative feeling takes away some of its power. It calms us and creates the space to remember what we know—that even though we're tired and rushed and cranky, our children are still precious and worthy of delight. Even if it's just for a moment, we can still stop and see them. During hard times, finding moments to acknowledge the wonder of this life will open you up to delight and will water your child's soul.

So name your tiredness. Name your fear. Name your frustration. Then give yourself permission to delight in this moment. You'll get back to the tiredness, the fear, the frustration in a minute. They deserve to have a hearing. But for now, put your phone away and make tiny spaces for joy. Listen to the song they wrote. Dance in the kitchen. Make a pillow fort and stay up late with your kids telling stories. If the night ends badly or milk spills all over the place, try not to let it defeat you. Get creative, look full into your children's faces, and whisper your love to them. They'll feel the freedom you're giving them, and you'll feel it too, as you release yourself into delight.

Reality Check

At the end of each of the needs chapters, you'll find a diagram and information to help you assess your responsiveness to that need. All the need diagrams, along with some practical strategies and exercises based on the needs, are also included in appendixes A and B at the end of this book.

As you consider the need diagrams, you'll probably find you are highly responsive to some needs and less responsive to others. To get a general idea of how responsive you are to the need for delight, look at the following diagram, and consider how prone you are to lean toward one side or the other. Consider asking your parenting partner, a friend, and/or your child to rate you as well. Differences in ratings are opportunities for insight and learning.

Delight

NEED TYPE: MIRRORING

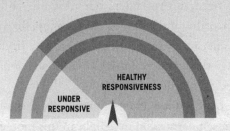

HEALTHY
RESPONSIVENESS

UNDER
RESPONSIVE

Here are some statements that may feel true if you tend to underrespond to the need for delight:

- I don't seem to really notice my child unless he is doing something wrong or bothersome.
- It's hard to think of times recently when I truly enjoyed my child.
- I generally feel agitated and annoyed at my child when I'm in her presence.

Here are some statements that may feel true if you are highly responsive to the need for delight:

- I enjoy spending time with my child, playing and discovering with them.
- I enjoy finding out how my child sees and experiences the world, even when it's different from my view or experience.
- I enjoy seeing what interests or motivates my child, even when those interests are different from my own.

Small Steps to Take Today

If you are someone who is highly responsive to the need for delight, celebrate! Pouring delight into our children builds foundations of security in them that they'll be able to stand on their whole lives.

And if you struggle at times with delight, like we do, will you spend some time thinking about why that might be? As you do, please release yourself from any feelings of guilt or shame that might well up within you, and remember we're all wired differently and have a range of life experiences that influence how we act in intimate relationships. Whatever your experiences, do you yourself feel worthy of love and delight? If not, could you sit with the idea that you are loved, just as you are? Beginning to truly believe this may set you free to love your children just as they are too.

Jeffrey sees a lot of parents who, for very legitimate reasons, have trouble delighting in and enjoying their children. Sometimes personalities clash, a developmental stage is incredibly difficult, or a life situation or diagnosis makes delighting hard. If this is the case for you, please give yourself permission to change the frame of delight. In the absence of an emotion that may be too hard to feel, consider what you can be *grateful* for about your child. Practice saying what you're grateful for about your child out loud to her. Your child needs to hear this from you, even if you're having trouble feeling it.

Sometimes it's hard to meet the need for delight because life has gotten too busy. Or we focus on the hopes and fears we have for our kids instead of on who they are as people in front of us right now. We can fall into the trap of believing that if we don't take every opportunity to correct and direct our kids, they'll miss out or be rejected or fail somehow. If this is how you're feeling, remember you're on a journey with your child that will last a lifetime. There will be plenty of time to guide your child to get where she needs to go, and we'll talk a lot about ways to do that in the next chapters.

So today, let's remember that life is a gift, this day is a gift, and your child is a gift. And there are no promises for tomorrow, no matter how hard we work. Even if it's just for a moment, will you take a deep breath and allow yourself to be still and be with your kid? With no agenda or judgment, let's try to really see our kids, just as they are, and let them know that we're glad they are here.

SUPPORT: HOW CAN I HELP?

Anticipating the Obstacles and Opportunities

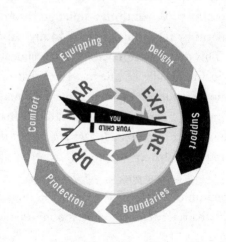

73

AMY

The Year of Much Baking

When I was a child, I baked with my mother. Chocolate chip cookies were our favorite thing to bake together, but I also remember scooping gooey brownie batter into a buttered pan, folding rolls into fancy shapes, and even dropping homemade doughnuts into piping hot oil. When our flat white circles of dough bobbed up puffy and golden, it felt like magic. Being in a warm, fragrant kitchen with people I love has always felt like home to me. I want my kids to know this feeling too, so ever since the boys were tiny, I've invited them into the kitchen.

I'm a precise recipe follower, which can make baking with small children a bit of a challenge. Still, when the boys were little, our baking sessions were mainly great. The guys and I all loved pulling out recipe books together to decide what to make, then gathering our bowls and ingredients to begin. As we worked, the boys did a fairly good job of taking turns and sharing tasks as long as I helped them navigate the process. Sometimes I did have to hold my own hands to keep myself from jumping in too quickly to guide and direct their efforts. When things didn't go according to plan, I managed my alarm by repeating a mantra to myself: *It's the process, not the product.* This mantra reminded me I was choosing to be here with my kids in the middle of our mess and that our experience together was more important than what we were making.

Half the flour we'd carefully measured didn't make it into the bowl? Time to whisper to myself, *It's the process, not the product.*

Wild stirring led to batter slopping all over the counter? *It's the process, not the product, it's the process, not the product.*

Egg dropped onto the floor? Random and unexpected whack of brother with batter-filled wooden spoon? *Process not product! Process not product!*

Mantras can really get you through sometimes.

As Josh grew older, his interest turned to other things, but our middle boy, Drew, caught the baking bug. By third grade he wanted to move beyond baking with my help to baking by himself and making up recipes on his own. At first I tried to stay in the kitchen with him while he worked, but watching him haphazardly throw heaping spoonfuls of baking powder, baking decorations, various cocoas, and oils into bowls was a little too painful. I decided that mantras can only carry you so far. It was time to come up with a plan.

Drew wanted to use the kitchen without my supervision, but he also loves being with people, so he asked if he could invite his neighborhood friends over to bake with him. I agreed that would work once or twice a week but told him that a really messy kitchen would be stressful for me. He promised that he and his friends would clean up after themselves. We also agreed that I would be the only one allowed to get things into and out of the hot oven when other kids were over, and Drew had to let me know when we were out of ingredients so I didn't get stuck with an empty pantry.

With that, Drew's afterschool baking sessions began. The neighborhood kids were eager to join in, so soon our tiny kitchen was packed with two or three additional minibakers, as well as an occasional brother. Sometimes the kids collaborated on a recipe, but usually they each grabbed their own bowl to bake from a cookbook, an online recipe, or their imagination as they saw fit. They made up a fancy name for their baked creations—*Fouchee Francais's*—and ooohhed and ahhed as I pulled their piping hot pans from the oven. Typically they would then try a few bites of what they'd made, sometimes grimacing in disgust, then run off to play something else.

Working from home, I quickly realized that the best way to get through the Great Baking Season of 2015 was to close my office door and try not to listen too closely to what was happening in the kitchen. I could appear when the kids needed me and disappear for the rest, which seemed to work well for all of us.

Every time Drew baked with his friends, our kitchen took on a flour-smeared covering of grime that the kids never really got clean, though they truly did try. Their baked creations usually sat on our counter for a day or two before I threw them away in the midst of rewiping the kitchen. Jeffrey does our family's grocery shopping, and more than once during this season, I saw his eyes grow wide when he read over our weekly list. "More flour? Really? And more butter?? Wow." Yep.

After about a year of afternoon baking sessions, Drew wholeheartedly considered himself a baker. And he was. He'd even learned how to make up some recipes on his own, though he told me his baked goods seemed to taste better when he followed directions.

Last year before my birthday, I found an online picture of a cake that looked amazing. Featured on a professional baking website, it was three layers tall and frosted with a rich, creamy filling, then covered with dark chocolate ganache. I showed the picture and recipe to the boys and asked them what they thought. "That looks awesome, Mom. Want us to make it for you?" I did. I picked up the ingredients, walked away from the kitchen, and they baked me a beautiful cake.

Support isn't always as clear cut as this, of course. Sometimes our kids need more structure, or it's harder to let go. But when it works—when we get to see them grow to master a skill on their own—natural child development can feel magical. This type-A mama is learning to get out of the way.

I had another thought as I wrote this story, and I'll share it in case it is encouraging to you too. I've sometimes felt bad that we haven't been able to afford to send the boys to as many camps or enrichment activities as I've seen other kids go to. I've wondered if they've missed out. But while I know Drew would have enjoyed a baking camp, I also wonder if the time he invested in learning to do something he enjoys on his own is more valuable than any weeklong class we could have signed him up for. His trial and error—literally pans and pans of inedible dishes—has given him the confidence to try new skills and the knowledge that he can work things out on his own. That kind of mastery only comes with time. Knowing this gives me one more reason to breathe and release myself into the joy of being in relationship with my kids. I choose to trust that they are becoming exactly who they are meant to be and believe that what I have to offer them is more than enough.

JEFFREY

An infant persistently reaches for something just outside her grasp, a three-year-old presses down on the pedals of a tricycle stuck in place, and a five-year-old struggles to sound out words on a page. An eight-year-old wants to play big sister's game but doesn't understand the rules, an eleven-year-old tangles a fishing line, a fourteen-year-old asks for help preparing for a talent show, and a seventeen-year-old wrestles with sorting out college applications.

Across all your child's stages of development, you will see the need for support. What your child sees and hears when they turn to you for collaboration and help in the moments when they need assistance—your body language and the words you speak—send powerful messages that shape not only how they understand themselves and their place in the world but what they will continue to pursue, and how. We are mirrors showing them who they are and what they are capable of.

Support: What It Is and Why It Matters

Support, a natural outgrowth of delight, is an exploration-side need on the compass. When we delight in our children, we enjoy them as they are. When we support them, we move into partnership and action as they move forward into the world in different ways. Support gives us the opportunity to help our kids discover and pursue the particular, intrinsic things they find interesting and valuable. It also gives us the opportunity to introduce important tasks they will need to master to succeed in life. Through support, we partner with our children as they learn about the world and find their place in it.

All of us are born with a wellspring of inner motivation to explore, discover, play, master, and share what we find. This innate curiosity and pursuit is powerfully wired into us. It is a defining feature of our humanity and is the reason why we have thoroughly filled nearly every niche on this planet and developed technologies that have taken us up to the moon and down two miles below the sea. Children have a whole world of possibilities to discover between the time they are born and when they set off on their own. They also have a whole world of challenges to face. These challenges may not be as intrinsically rewarding to meet, but they are still worth facing with effort, persistence, and courage.

Imagine you and your child are hiking through a native forest together, finding your way. Your child might run a little way in front of you and then come back to report excitedly about a stream to cross or a boulder to climb. When you support your child in instances like this—when they've encountered something they want to pursue or a new skill they want to master—you listen to their report and follow their lead, going with them to share in their excitement and anticipation. At other times, you take the lead on the trail by pointing out obstacles in your way that are necessary to tackle. You point out a hill that must be climbed or a path that has to be cleared to reach a worthwhile destination.

When we support our children by teaching them necessary skills or guiding them through the next stage of development, our support gives them a picture of the challenge ahead and tells them about the rewards beyond it. We can ask them their thoughts and feelings about the challenge and communicate our confidence that they're ready to take it on. We can even give them options for how to tackle what's to come, empowering them to find their own unique solutions.

What I Most Want You to Know about Support

Amy and I want our children to discover their natural-born gifts and talents, to grow in wisdom and knowledge and competence, and to contribute to the world in meaningful and life-giving ways. Researchers describe a human being's natural impulse to do all this as "autonomy seeking," which is the process of coming to see yourself as your own person with a particular set of values, aspirations, capacities, and beliefs.[1] People who develop a healthy sense of self over time are found to be more persistent and creative. And they've been shown to perform at a higher level because they believe they are living at harmony with their own interests, values, and abilities.[2]

The Elements of Healthy Support

Children who are on this path toward autonomy receive support from adults in distinctive ways, ways that researchers are increasingly able to quantify and describe. Parents support their child's healthy sense of self by (1) valuing their personal interests, feelings, and perspectives, (2) providing choices for them when reasonable, and (3) creating structure that allows them to experience success.[3] Doing these things helps children to develop competence and confidence pursuing goals, solving problems, and seeking help when needed.

1. **Valuing:** *taking your child's interests, feelings, and perspectives seriously.* The first important element of support is that you take your child's interests, feelings, and perspectives seriously. Your child may be fascinated with lizards, preoccupied with slime, and really want to know why the sky is blue. He may insist on doing everything himself or want you to stand right next to him to help him complete what you see as a simple task. You value rather than diminish him

when you take time to listen, respond, and ask questions about his lived experience, remembering that everything in life is new to him, even if it's old and ordinary to you.

Valuing means we take the time to solicit our children's views of the problems and opportunities they face. Often, as adults, we quickly form an adult perspective on a challenge our child encounters and want to impose a solution without taking the time to gather information from our child's perspective. Rather than asking what the problem is in our child's eyes, helping our child identify their thoughts and feelings about a situation, or asking our child what they think they need, we shoot quickly to *You just need to do this!* or even *Just let me do it for you!*

Asking *How would you like me to help you?* is a powerful statement to a child. It communicates that she has a right to some level of sovereignty over the things that affect her life, even if she might not have absolute say about what happens. And having taken the time to solicit her views, you can also take time to explain things from your perspective in language she can understand. This invites your child into your mind by sharing your thoughts and feelings, including your expectations and limitations for help. Valuing in this way is not about doing whatever your child wants but is simply taking the time to acknowledge that she is her own person with her own view of things.

2. **Choice:** *giving our children the opportunity to choose their own way and level when possible and appropriate.* The second key element of healthy support flows from valuing. Providing choices involves giving our children opportunities to choose their own way and level when it's appropriate rather than always dictating what and how they should do things simply because we can. Giving your child a choice can be as simple as asking them where they want to go on a bike ride instead of just picking a park yourself. If you see them struggling with something, ask, *Do you want me to help you with that, or do you want to try it yourself?* rather than moving in to take over.

This can be hard to do, especially if you are invested in a particular outcome and know you could force your way. Power is easy to wield if you have it, but it comes at a cost in relationships. Offering choices acts as a check on this natural human tendency to use power simply because it's ours. It also gives us the opportunity to become more aware of our own needs and pressures so that our parenting might become more mindful and intentional rather than reactive and arbitrary.

From the outside, letting children do things their own way will often look inefficient. Things might not look the way you would like them to. So for many of us, providing choices means taking a deep breath and valuing a process of learning over fixed results. If you are willing to surrender your ideal outcome in a situation, you can build your relationship with your child by framing the options that are reasonable to pursue, insisting on follow-through, and creating a process of self-evaluation. After an experience is over, a parent who values choices may ask their child questions like: "So, how did that work out? What could you have done differently? What do you need to think about for next time?"

3. Structure: *shaping the kinds of worlds we want to open up for our children.* The third essential element of healthy support is providing structure. At the most basic level, a child needs opportunity and exposure to fully develop their abilities and interests. Opportunity and exposure often depend on loving adults who have the means to create or facilitate opportunity. As parents, we have tremendous power to shape the kinds of worlds we open up for our children. Taking a child to the library, a park, or a museum are meaningful and powerful choices. Likewise, taking a child with you to work, to a nature reserve, to a city council meeting, or to visit a nursing home opens up worlds of nature, imagination, and community for them to explore. These are worlds that may one day be shaped by your child in ways you can't imagine.

We can also provide structure when the world becomes difficult and challenging for our children. Our children need us to help discern what they should attempt. Is a challenge in front of them too difficult? Too easy? Knowing your child will give you a sense of what goals make sense for them. Developmental psychologists have a term called "zone of proximal development."[4] This is the zone where your child is challenged enough to keep things interesting but not so challenged that they become discouraged. Knowing whether your child is inside the zone or has gone outside it depends on your coming alongside to observe and ask good questions. If your child is truly struggling to manage certain tasks, supportive structure takes the form of advocacy with someone like a doctor or teacher to more carefully evaluate what may be holding your child back.

When your child is in the "zone" where he is challenged but not overwhelmed, supportive structure is as straightforward as providing the practical tools, insights, and assistance he may need to work his way through a problem or task. For instance, if your child asks to sew a project on his own but you're not sure if he can handle the whole thing, you might say, *You have the instructions and materials to sew the stuffed animal. Do you think you'll need help with measurements or cutting? Come get me and let me know if you do.* When your child flounders, you can demonstrate instead of lecture and offer your help instead of taking over or throwing up your hands in frustration. We can teach our kids how to solicit help when they need it by making suggestions about where to go and whom to go to when they are stumped. And remember that learning takes repetition for mastery. We are giving support when we repeat things over and over, even after we think our kids should've already "gotten it."

Many parents fall into the trap of assuming that with proper instructions and indications of having the physical ability to do something, their child should be able to do things on her own. But this neglects the emotional capacities a child may have, which can vary significantly day to day and even hour to hour. Sometimes our children (especially younger children) just need us to do a task *with* them. Working independently is very much an adult value and capacity. Children, in contrast, often need connection to keep them motivated and encouraged as they explore and work. So if your child seems overwhelmed by a task you think they can handle, like putting away her clothes "where they belong," try saying something like, *Ok! I know the clothes pile looks big, but I bet you can do it. Why don't you put away five things and then I'll put away five things and then we can switch off again. We'll get this done in no time.* By your side, your child will grow in competence until it becomes natural for her to handle such tasks on her own.

Dopamine and Connection: What Does Your Child See When They Look into the Mirror of Your Eyes?

Studies of the brain have uncovered a biological element pushing us forward into exploration: the chemical dopamine. Dopamine has been dubbed "the pleasure-seeking neurotransmitter" because it gives us the feeling of being on the verge of a reward as we seek out new things.[5] Your child's hunger for discovery lies in their brain's dopamine network because dopamine provides motivation for seeking out potentially rewarding actions.[6] Dopamine drives us to understand cause and effect and to see how we can influence those effects. Thanks to dopamine, we crave to see what's around the next bend and what happens when we drop rocks into a stream or push cheerios off the high chair. We naturally ask ourselves, *What happens next? What am I capable of?* and *Where can I find joy in this world?*

Dopamine also drives your child to connect. As social beings, the greatest natural reward for humans is to share our discoveries and accomplishments with one another. When we say, "Look what I did!" we long to see a delighted, engaged response. When our children set out to discover the world, they are naturally going to look back to us to show us what they have found, because their brains light up when they see us reacting with delight and excitement at their conquests and discoveries. Your child does not have a way of understanding who they are without seeing their identity first reflected through you. You are their first mirror—that's the power of connectedness. Your reactions help push them forward to keep finding out who they are and their place in the world.

What do you reflect back to your child? Delight, shared interest, useful feedback and structure that open up greater possibilities? Or are you prone to reflect disinterest, displeasure, and criticism? Or worse, condemnation, punishment, and the withdrawal of support?

The answer to this mirror question could depend on your view of your child's natural path of development, a view that you may have never even consciously thought through. Some parents intuitively trust that their children will eventually grow, mature, and integrate themselves with the world around them as long as they have basic opportunities for stimulation, learning, nurture, and structure. Scientists call this attitude *organismic trust*.[7] We'll call it **growth trust**. And for good reason. Our survival requires that this growth happen!

Opposite this is a darker view of human development, the root of which is the idea that a child is naturally inclined to resist growth and maturity and so has to be poked, prodded, and forced to grow up and effectively integrate with the world around them. We'll call this **growth distrust**.

The reality is that most parents look at their children and can see evidence for both points of view. There are times when your child seems to graduate spontaneously to a new level of ability, understanding, and collaboration with those around him. There are also times when you look at your child and think, *Things haven't changed one bit from six months ago!* If your gut holds to a growth view, when you see your child reach a new stage of development, you'll think, *Well, isn't that lovely! It was just a matter of time. Hooray for her!* You'll look at the times when she doesn't seem to be moving forward and think, *Well, this has been a tough spell, but I know she'll get through it. I just need to keep supporting her until she gets over the hump. These things take time.*

But if your gut leans in the direction of growth distrust, you see new maturity or development and think, *Whew, it's about time. If I hadn't been keeping on him all this time, he surely would never have gotten here. Now I need to make sure he doesn't slip backward!* And you'll look at periods of stagnant development and think, *Ugh! If I don't figure out some way of getting through to him soon, he's never going to get where he needs to be.*

If you stop to think about it, most people manage to become adults capable of navigating the world, providing for themselves, and contributing to society in meaningful ways, even when their childhood circumstances have been less than optimal. You yourself may be one of those stories of overcoming, of pursuing goals and achieving them in spite of inadequate or inconsistent role models and support. History shows that humans are, if nothing else, resilient. And in some cases, it is not until things get hard that certain growth is even possible. It is good to remember this basic fact.

Furthermore, it helps to be reminded that while development happens naturally, it does *not* happen in a straight line. Think about your child's height. There are periods when they don't seem to grow at all, then sudden stretches when they grow like weeds. Likewise, many a book-loving parent has despaired over their child who isn't reading like the others in their class, only to see that same child suddenly become a chapter-book reader in the course of a few months. An anxious parent may worry that their early adolescent isn't making eye contact with adults and mumbles replies when questioned. Two years later this same teen may suddenly be able to hold a confident dinner conversation with guests. Growth happens naturally but unevenly.

Embracing a growth trust view gives you breathing room to be curious, patient, and kind toward your child. It allows life to be a windy course rather than a straight highway. Even if your child looks to you for support more than you think she should, takes longer to learn something than you wish she would, or is interested in things that seem frivolous to you, growth trust reassures you that your kid will get where she needs to go eventually. Growth trust creates space to be still and observe and not to react as if the fate of your child's future is hanging in the balance *right now*. Growth trust will show on your face. It will be present in the tone of your voice and the words you use. When things are hard, the mirror you turn toward your child will show him that he isn't a failure, a disgrace, or a bad kid. Even if he is stuck or made a mess or is behind his peers. The mirror, instead, will show that he is loved and not alone and that others have been in this place too and that he doesn't have to be afraid to try and fail or to make mistakes or to be different. Help is a normal thing to ask for and reasonable to receive because learning and growth matter more than achievements and trophies, and life is not a competition.

In the end, choosing to embrace a growth trust mind-set will make it easier to embrace the elements of support that research says contribute to greater competence, self-confidence, empathy, and connectedness with others. Trusting that your child is wired to grow and mature makes it easier to value your child's experience and explain your own more fully, to use your power more thoughtfully by offering choices, and to provide structure rather than take over.

The Freedom of Letting Go

As I've worked with parents over the years, there is a case that I have seen over and over again. Devout, concerned parents bring their adolescent to see me because their child is angry, disobedient, and engaging in unhealthy behaviors. The parents have consistently and fearfully raised their child to attend church, avoid unethical influences, and know right from wrong. Now things seem to be falling apart, and they are coming to terms with the fact that their power is all but gone. Lectures, inducements, and punishments no longer have much effect over the situation, but the parents' fears keep them from surrendering and letting their child go their own way completely. Because I speak their language of faith while also being a psychologist, they hope that somehow I will provide some miraculous God-ordained parenting solution to their problem or develop some God-inspired influence over their child that will cause them to start making the life choices the parents want them to make.

Another case that comes to me repeatedly is similar in origin but looks very different. A young adult comes to me anxious, depressed, and self-critical, having grown up in a family with devout parents who have raised them in an environment closely resembling the one described above. They followed the path of obedience, and their identity is firmly rooted in the narrow parameters set out for them through their adolescence into adulthood. But the identity formed strongly for them by their parents isn't working for them anymore, and the confusion and conflict they are experiencing as they question who they really are has become paralyzing. Because I speak their language of faith while also being a psychologist, they hope that somehow I can provide some magical God-derived inspiration that will set them free from feeling trapped and at war with themselves.

To both the parents in the first case and the young adult in the second case, I often find myself returning to a story that they are usually familiar with, Jesus's story of the prodigal son. In this story, the son of a rich father decides that he is through with living his father's life and demands his inheritance early so he can leave his father's home and build a life all his own. The term *prodigal* means "wastefully extravagant," and this is what the son in this story is. He sets out and foolishly and extravagantly spends all that his father has given him. Destitute, he returns home to discover that his father has been waiting for him the whole time. The story says that while the son was still far off, the father saw him and ran to meet him with arms of love open wide, celebrating his return.

While it is easy to place the wayward son at the center of the story, I redirect their attention to the father character. Jesus is telling us about the heart and nature of God. And in this telling, God is clearly an irresponsible father. Or so it would seem to some. This father knew his son's adventures would end in disaster and dishonor, even as he sent his impulsive son on his way into a world he wasn't ready for, with an inheritance that was outrageous for him to demand. Surely love doesn't look like that. Unless that is exactly what it looks like.

Love demands giving others the freedom to find out for themselves who they are and what they are capable of. Love is confident enough to trust that within each of us is a compass that will ultimately point us back to what is good, if we have been shown goodness. And love is extravagant enough to rejoice, rather than reprimand, the beloved's return, even when that return is one of disappointment and failure.

When I suggest to parents that they may need to change their focus from control and condemnation to an attitude more like the father in Jesus's story, many parents feel sad and afraid. Like the prodigal father, they see where this is likely to lead, and the pain is often too great for them to accept. So they go on searching for ways to force their children to change course. Some are brave enough to begin to share their fears—rather than their judgments—with their children. They begin listening to their children and asking them what support would look like to them. And often a universal deep longing to be seen and loved unconditionally kicks in just in time for their child to step back from the edge of some of the worst choices they were contemplating. But it is scary work for everybody.

When I suggest to the young adult in the case above that their heavenly parent sees them with this radically uncontrolling love, it can be just as scary. They worry that God isn't really like that and that the doors to God will be barred behind them if they move away from the God they have been taught to know. But then I've seen joy emerge when my clients take the chance and set out to find who they really are, what they truly value, and what they are good at apart from the judgments of those attempting to speak for God. Taking a risk on such an extravagantly loving and uncontrolling God often opens them up to unimagined possibilities of creativity, work, and meaning in their lives. They discover that God has placed within them the ability to discern for themselves what is good and holy and that grace is present with them through seasons of confusion and even willful self-destruction. The joy that flows from that discovery often leads to a love and worship that had previously escaped them and even seemed impossible.

There is so much to show our kids and so much we can do for them. They need our wisdom, knowledge, and structure sometimes. But if we want them to find their true path and develop the confidence to master obstacles and challenges, we need to be willing to get out of their way sometimes. We need to let them make mistakes, fall short, and generally make a mess of things. Remember that there's a desire in all of us to find our way back when we get lost and to move on when we get stuck in a rut. When our kids know they can trust us, they'll come back to us for support when they need it, eager to show us all they've discovered along the way.

Reality Check

To get a general idea of how responsive you are to the need for support, look at the diagram below, and consider how prone you are to lean toward one side or the other. Consider asking your parenting partner, a friend, and/or your child to rate you as well. Differences in ratings are opportunities for insight and learning.

Support

NEED TYPE: GUIDANCE

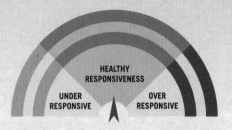

Here are some statements that may feel true if you tend to underrespond to the need for support:

- I prefer to let my child figure things out on his own.
- I am often too busy with my own work and activities to give much time to helping my child with theirs.
- When I try to help my child with something, I often end up feeling frustrated and walking away.

Here are some statements that may feel true if you tend to overrespond to the need for support:

- I am quick to jump in and show my child how things are done.
- I often take over a task for my child if I feel like he's not doing it right.
- I am really uncomfortable with the idea of my child failing or not reaching his full potential.

Small Steps to Take Today

If you feel like you may be a little undersensitive to the need for support in your child, don't pressure yourself to know how to do that perfectly. Our kids don't need us to have all the answers or solve all their problems. More than anything, they benefit when we're being curious *with* them and when we help them consider problems in new ways. Your child just needs you to see him and take the time to say, "How can I help you?" or "Look what you discovered!"

If you feel like you may be oversensitive to the need for support, remember that children close doors to whole worlds when they feel stupid, inadequate, or unnecessary. When we take over for them or insist that they do things perfectly, we send them the message that their efforts are not good enough and take away their motivation to try. The key to healthier support is to focus less on the end product and more on the process. Your child needs your help to set her own goals, evaluate her own effort, and judge her own outcomes. Ask her what role she wants you to play in helping her get where she wants to go, and try to step away if she wants to do something on her own.

6

BOUNDARIES: HOW FAR IS TOO FAR?

Defining and Valuing Limits

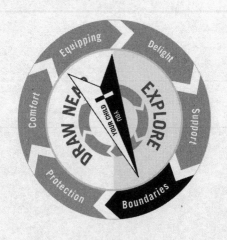

AMY

Stolen Legos and Neighborhood Flares

One of my bright-eyed, tow-haired boys tugged on my sleeve, pulling me down to sit with him on the sofa. I listened as he stammered over his words. Slowly, the story came out—his brother, our first grader, had been stealing Legos from his classroom and bringing them home to add to our boys' personal collection. I hugged my guilt-ridden reporter and told him it was brave of him to tell me and that I would handle it from there.

That night at bedtime, I took our first grader aside to tell him I knew that there were some Legos in our Lego tub that didn't belong to us. Could he explain to me how they got there? Confronted, he confessed everything. Yes, he had been taking Legos from his classroom. His teacher had brought in a big bin for everyone to play with, and some of the pieces were so cool that he had brought them home to keep for himself. He knew it was wrong, but he had wanted those Legos so badly.

I reminded him that when he had taken those pieces for himself, he had taken them away from his teacher and his class. Could he imagine how he would feel if someone came to our house and snuck away with his Lego pieces? Then I asked how he thought he could make this right. Sniffling, he told me he would gather up the pieces he'd stolen and return them to the class Lego bin the next day. I nodded, agreeing this was a good start, but I also wanted him to put together a collection of his own favorite pieces to give to the class and to apologize to his teacher for his theft. I told him I believed everything would be okay, but only after he worked to repair what he had done.

My boy sobbed with worry. "They're going to kick me out of school!" he wailed. "And how did you know about those stolen pieces, anyway?" As he gathered the Legos together, I told him sometimes mamas just know things, then reassured him again that

I believed everything would be okay. He crawled, shaking, onto his top bunk, and his cries followed me as I walked downstairs. A huge part of me wanted to let him call his teacher right then to put an end to his misery.

"Ugh, is this okay?" I asked Jeffrey as we stood together in the kitchen, listening to him cry.

"Honestly, I think it's the best thing that could happen to him," Jeffrey replied. Our boy had a long, hard night of soul-searching ahead of him, one we were sure he would remember. But better that he learn a lesson like this now, before he faced something with much higher stakes.

I did call his teacher then to prepare her for our son's confession the next morning. She chuckled as I explained the situation. "Ah, I have noticed the level of Legos in my bin going down. But please tell him not to worry about it! I think a lot of the boys are taking Legos home with them. It's probably to be expected, with me putting them out there in the classroom like that." I thanked her for being understanding but asked her to please join me in taking his stealing seriously. When he came in the next morning to confess, it was important to me that she not dismiss his wrongdoing.

As we walked the short distance to school the next day, my boy took every step slowly, as if walking to his own execution. "Do you have the Legos?" I asked, and he nodded miserably, holding up the bag. "Okay, then. I'm here with you, and I know you're brave enough to speak for yourself. Ready?" He swallowed and pushed the door open to walk toward his teacher. As promised, she was right there waiting for him.

His teacher and I stood silently for several long moments, waiting for him to gather the courage to speak. Finally, he whispered, "I stole some Legos. I'm sorry. I brought them back and some of mine too." As he handed over his bag, his teacher knelt down to address him directly.

"Thank you for apologizing. I forgive you, and I'm glad you

brought the Legos back. These Legos belonged to my sons, and I like having them in the classroom for us all to play with, don't you?" He nodded, and I saw a spark of life return to his anguished frame.

"Okay, well do you want to stay here and wait for class to start or go outside and play with your friends?" she asked.

"Can I stay here and play with Legos?"

"Of course," his teacher replied. He glanced at me with a relieved smile before taking off to dump his bag of pieces into the communal Lego bin. Now that he'd addressed his mistake, he was free to play.

Our boundaries story could end there. It's clean and tidy, right? *Thou shalt not steal, and if thou dost stealeth, thou shalt haveth consequences.* But this Lego incident actually prompted some deeper conversations about the boundaries and behavioral expectations we were setting for the boys. Jeffrey and I know that they, like all people, are born explorers. They are made to push limits and to want more—desiring and overcoming are some of the most thrilling parts of being human. But sometimes their desiring goes too far, pushing them to do things that could hurt them or other people. So we want to find a balance between encouraging their exploration and teaching them the value of safe, respectful limits. Like David sang in Psalm 16, we want to *set their boundary lines in good places so their walk will be secure.*

We decided that when it's clear that a line has been crossed, like in the Lego incident, it is wise to be firm with our consequences. But we also looked hard at ourselves and realized that some of the boundaries we set for our kids were based only on rules we'd been given ourselves as kids and on the high value we place on our own peace and quiet. That's not necessarily a bad thing—to keep a house with three little boys running without too much chaos, it's reasonable to establish a bit of order. But sometimes we powered up just to get them out of our way, doing things like snapping at them for begging for snacks around dinnertime, when they were most hungry. And by overcorrecting their small, normal childhood behaviors, we not only risked shaming them for being themselves but also making the important times we needed to discipline them less meaningful.

We also did a lot of sheltering of the boys, blocking them off from media and conversations that dealt with hard issues. We kept their world small and safe, which was probably one reason why things like their Lego collection felt so important to them. But we wanted the boys to grow up believing that their lives could tell a big story. If we kept their vision small, we wondered if the only way they would think to expand it would be in sneaky ways, like stealing from a toy bin. Wouldn't it be better to start opening up the world to them early, even by introducing hard topics in thoughtful ways, so they could learn to navigate difficult things alongside us? Expanding their world might help the boys see why we need to set limits in the first place.

Jeffrey and I realized that if we didn't make some shifts, our boundaries could begin to feel like a cage to our kids, hemming them in place and setting our relationships up for distance and conflict. But was I brave enough to push my kids on to courage, purpose, and a life of adventure, even outside my own comfort zone? Only if I believed that Love is all over the map, calling us to push back some branches and follow new trails.

Our kids' hunger for more could push them out into the world in beautiful ways if we'd let it. Or at least that's what Jeffrey and I told ourselves when the boys were two, seven, and nine and we decided to bring them with us to Washington, DC, to participate in a march against human trafficking. We wanted them to see us standing up for a societal boundary we believe in—that people should not be bought and sold. We also hoped to show them that acting on behalf of others can point us to purpose and can clarify the way we think about our own wants and needs. But when we arrived at the march's registration table, we wondered if we'd made a mistake. The previous year's walk had focused on international trafficking, and we'd prepped the boys for the event by telling them we'd be marching for "children trapped in trouble." But local stories from formerly enslaved sex workers would be the focus of our action this year, and the march signs being handed out displayed one of two bold, all caps messages: REAL MEN DON'T BUY SEX and YOUR DAUGHTER COULD BE NEXT.

Oh my. This wasn't what I had expected. As I stood still, thinking silently for a moment, Josh took in the scene as well. Not one to miss much, he tugged on my hand, beckoning me down to hear him whisper, "It's a good thing *we* don't have a daughter." He'd never experienced anything like this before, and his brain's first reaction was fear.

Before conscious thought, we all look for difference, evidence to separate us from others' pain. If we don't enter those moments of fear and consciously push beyond them, we risk closing ourselves off from one another. I was glad I was there by my boy's side, assuring him that even though this was new, he didn't need to be afraid.

The march organizers soon invited us to gather around a stage and listen as survivors shared their stories. One of the young women led us in a chant, and I looked at her and thought, *She's one of the daughters.* She was one of the daughters who was stolen. And now she was free and inviting us to join her work of rescue. I dared a long sideways look over to Jeffrey. Drew was pressed close to his side, and Nathan curled up in his arms. I wondered what they were all thinking. We were venturing into unfamiliar territory together.

Back home that night, we debriefed. The day had introduced the boys to some hard issues, but they were taking it in stride and embracing their new role as actors in a story of freedom. Well, except for Nathan, who had really just been in it for the snacks. We hoped Josh and Drew would remember the pain and the strength of the women who'd led us that day, the daughters of God who had opened up our world with their courage. We also wondered if perhaps we should get one of those signs to hang up on our wall, the way some people hang inspirational sayings. *Real Men Don't Buy Sex* seemed as reasonable a message as any to convey to a houseful of growing boys.

Sometimes I introduce my kids to painful concepts and then wonder if I've shared too much. Or we take them places and then worry we've pushed them too far. But I can tell you that orienting our lives to boundaries in this way seems to have taken the pressure off our own interpersonal grievances with one another. Our growing understanding of the world's very real suffering has put our family annoyances in perspective. The things that used to stress us don't seem to matter as much now. When one of the kids does something kids do, like start a pointless fight with his brother or snap at us or roll his eyes dramatically, we can usually just say, "Hey, you know we don't treat each other that way. Why don't you try again but this time in a kinder tone?" We try not to spend too much time on the behavior or make it a focus of anger or shame. Once our boy's moment of intensity has passed, he usually wants to turn himself around, anyway. Expanding our view seems to have given us all clearer vision.

This kind of redirection can still be exhausting. Trust me, I know. The neighborhood moms and I have joked that we need to set up a flare system of solidarity so we can send little color-coded rockets up into the sky whenever a small child is screaming inconsolably on the floor or someone bigger has stomped to a bedroom in tears. Then when things are hard, at least we could peer out our windows and think, *Oh look, the Thompsons are struggling right now too. And oof, there go the Washingtons. And the Turners! It is a bad night for us all.*

It helps to remember that we're not alone—kids struggle because they're kids and still growing. When Jeffrey and I take a deep breath and consider the big picture, we're not so reactive to our kids' rudeness and misbehaviors. This turns us all around much more quickly. There are some things worth taking seriously and some worth standing up for. For the rest, we're just going to keep reorienting ourselves to loving one another and trust that our kids will grow in that direction as they mature.

Our boys will spend the majority of their lives apart from us. As they journey on, they may be tempted or invited to enter small-minded spaces—places where they could use their position or power to take what they want and get away with it, at a deep cost to themselves or someone else. In those moments, they'll need confidence, conviction, and understanding that their actions matter, for good or for harm. I hope they'll feel the twist of the compass inside them, pointing them to boundaries set in good places. May they turn to different margins and yearn for something more.

JEFFREY

A two-year-old hits while screaming *no!*, a five-year-old sneaks extra sugary snacks, an eight-year-old whines relentlessly about an expensive toy, an eleven-year-old wants to watch a show you're not sure she's ready for, a thirteen-year-old talks back with disrespect, a fourteen-year-old sneaks out in the middle of the night, and a sixteen-year-old wants to wear a shirt you're not comfortable with.

Throughout our lives as parents, in ways large and small, our kids are going to show us that they need boundaries. They will likely also relentlessly question our boundary decisions. We need wisdom to consider which of our boundaries should stand and which need to be expanded as our kids grow and mature.

With delight and support, we take time to see, value, and enjoy our children as they are. We help them become more competent, confident, and creative versions of themselves, to go where *they* want and need to go. But our children are not the only ones in the world. They share this world with others, each of whom have equal value and are also worth being seen, delighted in, and supported. You—and your child's other family members, friends, and neighbors—also have places you want and need to go. Our children need boundaries because they need our help learning to understand and navigate this shared life space.

Boundaries: What They Are and Why They Matter

In the simplest of terms, a boundary is a dividing line. When someone crosses over a boundary, even if they are simply trying to find their own way, they have stepped into a danger zone or into the space of someone else. Continuing on and over the boundary may mean getting hurt or hurting someone else. Boundaries is the need to have limits—boundaries help our children understand that their actions can have painful consequences, both for them and for others.

As an adult, you've seen how your words and actions have affected your life and others, and how others' words and actions have affected you. You've seen consequences emerge over time, and you've learned to balance the needs of others against your own. Actions come easily for children, but they have a much harder time seeing and understanding effects. When we name or set boundaries we are teaching them that their actions have consequences. We can do that harshly or with grace, recognizing that effects are not always easy to see or understand. Especially when those effects are hidden or far off in the future and the part of your brain responsible for seeing things from the perspective of another or in the future are not fully formed. Our children's ability to recognize their own boundary lines emerges slowly over time. To gain this vision, they need our help understanding when the pursuit of their own needs is a healthy one or whether it goes too far.

We respond to our kids' need for boundaries for three reasons:

1. **To teach them how to live at peace with others and to understand that their actions have consequences.** Failure to master sharing space with others will have significant

consequences for your child and those around her as she grows.[1] An adult who is unable to anticipate, determine, or respect the needs, perspectives, and experiences of others is liable to become a bore at best and a tyrant at worst. No parent wants their child to become that person. And not only for the sakes of their future friends, spouse, children, coworkers, or employees. We don't want our child to become that sort of person for her own sake because we know the isolation, rejection, and suffering that will come to her from such a lack of other-awareness and respect.

2. **To pass on our values about the kind of family and society we want to be a part of.** Because we are human, we are inclined to value our own needs *above* others'. But if we become more mindful and intentional, we can make choices that honor ourselves *and* others. Setting healthy boundaries in your family that focus on mutual understanding and respect shows your children how to "do to others what you would have them do to you."[2] Healthy boundaries teach our children how to love themselves *and* their neighbors, first in their families and then in the wider world.

3. **And, finally, we give our children boundaries so that one day they will be able to set healthy boundaries for themselves.** When we refuse to be pressured or treated badly by our children, we model how people who respect themselves expect to be treated. When we do this without harshness, shame, or threats, we teach our children that they also deserve respect. If we model this consistently over time, our children will learn how to set boundaries respectfully and unapologetically for themselves.

In my work, families tend to come see me when they face two sorts of boundary issues. In the first, their family life has been taken over by long drawn-out scenes of parents pleading, and failing miserably, to coax their child to act civilly or to follow simple rules. In these families, boundaries are mushy and effectively optional. In the second case, family life is consumed by the naming and enforcement of rules and rewarding or punishing behavior accordingly. In these families, boundaries are rigid and paramount. In both cases, people are stressed out and miserable.

Parents and children in both types of families are wrestling with the need for healthy boundaries. And most of us, pushed to our limits long enough, have the potential to be both types of parents—the pleaders and the shut-it-downers. And most of us have natural inclinations to move in one direction or the other, especially under stress.

What I Most Want You to Know about Boundaries

For parents like the first ones I described, "the pleaders," there is often an unease or uncertainty about asserting authority over their children's lives. There are plenty of reasons why this might be the case. Some parents simply dislike conflict or are too exhausted to set and maintain boundaries. Some grew up with parents who were rigid or even cruel authoritarians, and experience the exercise of parental authority as controlling or even abusive. So they've decided not to impose limits or consequences on their children because of the pain they experienced growing up. Others had parents who were more like peers, so even if they sense that there is value in exercising authority, they have no healthy model for what that looks like.

If setting boundaries feels uncomfortable to you for any of those reasons, consider that there is a difference between treating your child with equal dignity and treating her with equal knowledge, wisdom, and maturity. Our children absolutely deserve equal dignity. Just as you are a fully formed individual separate from your own parents, children are individuals in their own right, and they should be treated as such. But our kids are not our equals in knowledge, wisdom, or maturity. So they need us to draw boundaries and insist on outcomes at times. Over time, they'll grow in maturity and self-control, and as they do, our need to manage their boundaries and behaviors can relax accordingly. But giving children equal authority when they are not ready for it actually creates anxiety for them.[3] Their brains are not developed enough to envision the consequences of their actions and demands, so without boundaries, they easily stumble into pain and create conflict in their lives and relationships. It's more compassionate to guide them than to leave them traveling blind.

For parents like those in the second type of family I described, the "shut-it-downers," setting boundaries is mainly an issue of discipline, and discipline for them is about teaching respect for authority by demanding obedience. For these parents, obedience is seen as an essential indicator of whether their child is on a good path or headed for trouble. And since parents have the power to control almost every aspect of their children's lives, we can greatly influence our kids' choices and behaviors this way, at least in the early years. But a child doing what authority figures demand purely out of fear or reward is not the same thing as a child slowly discovering his place in the world alongside others, or learning to think about which of his needs are worth pressing into and which go too far. Neither is obedience out of fear a sign that a child has genuine respect for others, because respect grows from admiration and from understanding the value and legitimacy of someone else's needs and experiences.

If forcing compliance through punishments and threats is our primary process, what we teach our children is that they should respect power, not people. They learn that if you have power, you get to make your own rules and ignore others' rules. *Because I said so*, *I don't want to hear it*, and *You look me in the eye when I'm talking to you* are all lines we can use on our kids to silence them, humiliate them, or force them to submit to us. With our words, actions, and facial expressions, we can demand obedience by making them feel how small and powerless they are. And our kids, who don't have our power, are left only with the choice to accept powerlessness or rebel against it.

A child who grows up with parents who use their power to enforce boundaries is an expert in power dynamics. He learns that when he has power, he doesn't have to share space unless he feels like it. She learns that when she doesn't have power, she has to submit to others or scheme for a way to get what she wants by some other means. What they haven't learned is how to share space with others on the basis of equal value and respect.

Embracing the Third Way

Between these two poles is a third way, a way that sees boundary setting and discipline not as a matter of power and immediate control but as a process that, with patience and persistence, gradually forms self-respect and concern for the needs and experiences of others. This sort of discipline emphasizes the process of developing awareness and self-control over time, alongside a parent who sees and understands things a child does not. Naming and setting healthy boundaries in this way creates the opportunity for our children to gradually learn how to balance their own needs with the needs of others and learn to live at harmony with themselves and the world.

Healthy boundaries are a gift, and they can bring more freedom to your family and grow your relationship with your child. In those moments of guilt when you are struggling with saying no to something you know is not good for your kid, I want you to understand the value of what you are offering when you give your child a boundary. And in other moments, when you are struggling with anger or feeling out of control about your child's choices, I want to give you tools for how to speak to that situation and encouragement to keep looking forward with hope.

Understanding Your Child's Brain Development

To set healthy boundaries and discipline without engaging in unhealthy power dynamics, it's important to understand how your child's brain functions and grows. It's also important to understand how much your child needs you and your mature brain for her own healthy development.

You and your child's brains have two systems for processing information, which we can call the thinking brain and the feeling brain. These two brains have totally different agendas and respond to information in entirely different ways.

The thinking brain is slow, linear, and dependent on words and concepts. It is heavily influenced by memories that tell a coherent story and can be applied logically for future situations, and it is often associated with a region of your brain called the prefrontal cortex.[4]

The feeling brain is fast, nonlinear, and sensory-based. It responds to nonverbal messages like tone, touch, sights, and smells and is most heavily influenced by emotionally charged and sensory-laden memory "snapshots," or memories that shape our gut reactions to events. The feeling brain is most often associated with a complex set of regions in the brain generally referred to as the limbic system.[5]

The agenda of the thinking brain, which relies on the logic of past situations and future possibilities, is to analyze and synthesize. *What just happened to me? How did that happen? What should I learn from that experience? In the future, how could I apply what I have learned? What is going on over there? Have I seen this before? How did it end last time I saw something similar? How should I use that information to guide what I do next?*

The agenda of the feeling brain, which relies on fast-charging sensory and emotional snapshots of previous experiences, is quite different. *Survive, now! Eat. Sleep. Mate. Fight. Run. If it feels good, move toward it. If it feels bad, get away from it or destroy it.*

An average, healthy adult's thinking and feeling brains are balanced together, like this:

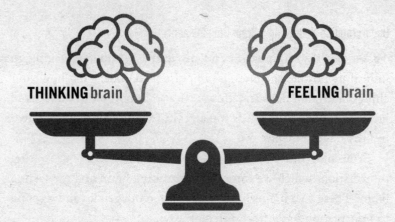

We all have moments when our wants, fears, or emotions get the best of us, but because both parts of our adult brains are fully developed, we're generally able to apply weight to either side of the scale when we find ourselves out of balance.

But a child doesn't start with a balanced scale. Children are mainly driven by their feeling brains, or limbic systems, so young humans start with plenty of capacity for processing the world emotionally but limited capacity for processing the world rationally. A child's information-processing scale is naturally weighted to the feeling side, like this:

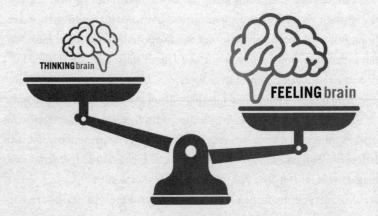

The feeling brain finishes up much of its development by pre-adolescence, making early childhood incredibly important for shaping how information is processed emotionally.[6] In contrast, the thinking brain takes its sweet little time to mature, finishing up most of its development by the early-to mid-twenties, and generally earlier in girls and later in boys.[7] It actually takes a dip in maturity during adolescence, which explains why when you ask a teenager in exasperation, "What were you thinking?" sometimes you are met with a blank stare. The honest answer to your question may be that he genuinely wasn't thinking.[8]

Let me pause here for a moment. Because the above information has astounding implications for your parenting. In fact, it has astounding implications for all your relationships. For now, sit with this idea that you have two brains and so does your child. And that these two brains you both have operate with very different agendas and respond to entirely different sources of information. Furthermore, your child is severely handicapped relative to you on the "thinking" side of the equation.

When your child has a want, their feeling brain is going to drive them to get it, regardless of the cost. In fact, children's thinking brains are often not developed enough to even consider the cost. And children can be very convincing, full of reasons why they should be able to have what their feeling brains are convinced they need. Parents who rely on harsh punishments may discover that, especially early on, they are able to shut down their children's misbehaviors and pleadings. But this isn't because their children are using their thinking brains and explicit memory systems to remember the logic of what their parents have taught them. No, they are using their feeling brains and implicit memories to remember the feeling of being physically or emotionally hurt. While the emotional memory of an angry lecture, painful swat, or harsh consequence may stop a child the next time he wants to misbehave, it won't help him remember what to do instead, and it may hinder his curiosity and development in the long run.

The Importance of Mapping Things Out

With an eye toward relationship and a long-view perspective, I believe it's much more important for a child to learn over time what to do in certain situations than to quickly learn what not to do. This kind of learning can be done only by walking through life with your children and mapping out a path with them. Such an approach follows the same principles that guide support: valuing, choices, and structure. In fact, boundaries are simply a natural extension and aspect of support, with the considerations of others' needs, perspectives, and experiences explicitly added to the equation.

One of the primary developmental differences between you as an adult and your child is that you have a fully developed thinking brain, so you can see things from multiple perspectives and across time. You remember how things have gone in the past, and you see what lies ahead, across a wide range of possibilities. You are able to step back and observe your thoughts and feelings while also imagining your child's thoughts and feelings from their perspective. This is called mentalizing.[9] With all this information in mind, you can determine a wise path forward.

In contrast, your child carries only fragments of information, mainly having to do with his immediate objectives. So we can avoid many conflicts and "boundary violations" when we take the time to name and explain expectations for what you and your child have to face together. This involves voicing what you can see in your mind about a situation, including what lies ahead in the future, and helping your child see beyond his immediate interests. By anticipating your thoughts, feelings, and choices to your child, and naming her potential thoughts, feelings, and choices, you help your child develop the ability to mentalize, or what Dr. Dan Siegel has called *mindsight*.[10] Mindsight is the ability to see into other people's minds and into the future to help determine your actions rather than simply being swept along by the moment. Mindsight is a mental map that gives your child a view of the trail ahead.

Going into Target? All your child is thinking about is what he can get there. Nothing else matters. And once you've experienced one or two trips to Target with a begging child, you can anticipate what is coming before you even walk through the doors.

If you're already there and engaged in a struggle with your child, consider what you need to accomplish and whether you have any flexibility to offer. If your no needs to stay no, talk through that in a way that allows your child's need to be valued, even if it can't be met immediately. "Hey, bud, I know how much you love going to the toy aisle. I don't have time today, but how about we make a date to come back when we have more time. I know it's disappointing." Or, "Yes, that cereal is so delicious, isn't it? We only buy it for special occasions, but when we get home, will you draw a picture of it for me and put it on the fridge so I don't forget to get it for you when it's time?"

Or if you can allow for a little more flexibility, you could say, "I tell you what, I know how much you love going to the toy aisle, but I only have twenty minutes. If we can get all my things in fifteen minutes, we can go to the toy aisle, but for only five minutes. What I'm worried about is that you're going to get really excited about some toy you see and start begging me to buy it. What do you think?" In this case, you are picturing, or mapping out, the future for your child by getting your child to picture and take ownership, ahead of time, for his future choices. Then you can map out for him what your choices are going to be depending on his actions. "Well, I tell you what. I'll take you over to the toys, but we're not buying anything today. You can put it on your birthday wish list, but we're not leaving with anything, got it? And if you do start asking me for something, then visiting the toy aisle isn't going to be an option next time we come to the store. We'll have to wait until your brain is better able to handle the excitement."

Even better, take a few minutes to map out a situation with your child before you enter it, and get her to understand and verbally agree to the plan. Before navigating a playdate, store, or school drop-off, sit in the car and talk through what's about to happen and how you would like things to go. Tell your child how long you anticipate you'll be there, whether or not you'll be staying with her, and some things to look out for while she's there. Come up with a little slogan she can say to confirm that she hears and understands what you said. She can repeat the plan back to you and then say, "Go team!" or "Got it."

Your child's boundaries can and should expand over time, so as your kid gets older and more mature, these mapping conversations can grow and get deeper. Before they set out into the world on their own, our children should have much more freedom to negotiate boundaries for themselves. They earn the privilege of expanding their boundaries as they show us that they know how to take other people's needs into account, as well as making responsible choices for themselves.

Natural and Restorative Consequences

As you navigate through life together, you'll have ample opportunities to offer your child natural consequences when they cross a boundary or make a poor choice. For instance, you and your kid may agree that he can do his chores on the weekend, as long as they're all done by bedtime on Sunday. If Sunday night comes and his chores aren't done, the next weekend he'll need to complete them before doing anything else on Friday night. If you've mapped this out ahead of time, this won't be a surprise because the two of you will have already agreed on consequences if he didn't follow through.

But there are other times when more serious breaches of trust and respect occur, breaches that require a more careful consideration of the boundaries you have with your child. In these cases, you'll need to reassess the privileges and trust you have given your child. Perhaps your child has broken boundaries having to do with her online activity, knowingly engaging with harmful material or purchasing things without permission. Perhaps your teenager has lied about his whereabouts on a weekend sleepover. Perhaps your child has written hurtful comments online about another peer or passed along inappropriate content. In such cases, serious conversations need to occur. Your goal should be to gather information, see things from your child's view, share how others may be experiencing the situation, including yourself, and seek reconciliation. This is how you can map a way forward with a clear affirmation of personal boundaries and expectations.

In more serious boundary breaches, it is valuable to our children to feel the weight of their actions and to work to regain trust and standing. There can be consequences that last beyond an uncomfortable conversation. But if you want to foster a positive learning experience, make the consequences as restorative and natural as possible. Your child may have to lose privileges until concrete signs of trust and responsibility have been reestablished. To make consequences tangible, you might insist that she work to repay someone, write out an apology, do community service, or research an issue, depending on the situation. In these cases, when things feel hard and even impossible, try not to despair. Remember *growth trust* and that your child's brain will do the work it needs to do to develop and organize itself to succeed in the world *with* others, especially if you walk with her to find a way forward when she seems lost in her mistakes.

A growth trust mind-set will help you embrace each of these strategies for thinking about and enforcing boundaries with your child because growth trust presumes that your child is invested in more than just getting his own way. It presumes that your child wants things to go well for him *with* others, not just for him alone. And this point of view is completely justified in light of the essential need all humans have to stay connected to others. Our genes tell us that rejection, especially by our caregivers, is an invitation to death. Our survival has always depended primarily on staying in the good graces of our clan. We may push the limits of rejection, but we don't want to go so far that we get kicked out. The urge to have our way is strong in all of us, but somewhere inside most every child is the desire for a win-win and for both of you to be happy with your experiences together.

If you find yourself powering up—relishing in a position of exerting power over your child or acting out a pattern from your childhood that taught you boundaries but left you feeling small— then I encourage you to rethink. Remember the call of relationship and that we give our children boundaries not to close them in and keep them under our control but to help them develop self-control and to direct them toward paths of healthy discovery and abundant life alongside others.

There is a promise that runs through the Judeo-Christian faith story. It's a promise that one day there will come a time when love toward neighbor will not be a rule that people follow out of guilt or fear but because it is written on their hearts. Some people believe that this promise will come to pass only in some future age, when God changes us in some sudden spiritual transformation. But perhaps such an age is available to us now, in the life and wisdom of the Spirit. If we let it, that Spirit will work through us to write the laws of love of self *and* others on our children's hearts as we do the hard and patient work of giving them the gift of healthy boundaries.

Reality Check

To get a general idea of how responsive you are to the need for boundaries, look at the diagram below, and consider how prone you are to lean toward one side or the other. Consider asking your parenting partner, a friend, and/or your child to rate you as well. Differences in ratings are opportunities for insight and learning.

Boundaries

NEED TYPE: TAKING CHARGE

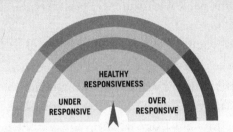

Here are some statements that may feel true if you tend to underrespond to the need for boundaries:

- I generally let my child have his own way.
- I tell my child what he can or can't do, but he does what he wants anyway.
- I go through periods of laying down the law but seem to have trouble following through.

Here are some statements that may feel true if you tend to overrespond to the need for boundaries:

- I have strong expectations and rules for how my child should act, and I enforce them.
- It is very important to me that my child learns to obey.
- I am willing to resort to severe punishment if my child is disobedient.

Small Steps to Take Today

If meeting the need for boundaries is a struggle for you, take heart. You are not alone. Boundaries may be the hardest need to meet consistently, and most parents go through periods of throwing up their hands. A child's ability to recognize and consider the consequences of his actions and the needs of others takes a long time to develop and master, and helping your child understand and respect boundaries can feel like an uphill struggle, even on good days. Try to approach this need with patience, perseverance, and grace for your child and yourself.

If you find yourself underresponding to your child's needs for boundaries, take time to remember why boundaries are so important. Boundaries equip our children to navigate the world with wisdom and safety and to build better relationships with others. Holding on to this knowledge will help you persist when your child is going through the death wails of having his unlimited free will constrained. Leave space for the wailing. It's part of the process. Surely you too have grieved that you couldn't do what you wanted, when you wanted, how you wanted.

If you find yourself on the overresponsive end of the spectrum, you likely already have a strong sense of the value and gift of boundaries. Now consider whether your approach to meeting the need for boundaries relies mainly on force and consequences. When children respond to boundaries only because of punishment or reward, they are unlikely to value and internalize those boundaries beyond the influence of those rewards and punishments. Take time to slow down and understand what is going on inside your child that makes some boundary a challenge. Is he hungry? Tired? Anxious? Overexcited? Distracted? Rather than going straight to consequences, say "Try that again, bud," or "Are you forgetting something?" If something persists, ask, "Will you help me understand what you're feeling right now?" Other times, be willing to redirect the focus of your relationship away from minor boundary violations. Don't let small offenses consume your relationship. If the same boundary issues keep resurfacing, consider that your child may not yet be fully capable of meeting your expectations or your expectations may need to be adjusted. Her brain may need to mature, or she may need added support to meet your boundary more consistently. Children with ADHD, for instance, have a very hard time inhibiting their behavior in the heat of the moment even though they know the rules and the consequences.

AMY

One Final Exploration

On that long-ago day at the antihuman trafficking walk, Jeffrey and I lingered until sunset, meeting new friends and learning more about the good work of the organizations gathered there. As the last band played, the boys found a folded table lying on the ground and turned it into a dance floor. From a distance, I watched their feet move to the music and felt at peace. In spite of all we had seen and heard that day, we were still there in the moment, together, with music and joy. With delight, support, and boundaries, we can explore all there is in the world and all there is in ourselves, and find much reason to dance.

PROTECTION: ARE YOU SAFE?

Resolving to Protect from True Harm

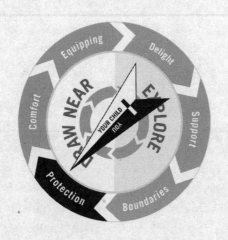

AMY

Alligators, Strangers, and Fear

So many things in life are beyond our control and even beyond our imagination. I think about that whenever I read an article about a tragedy involving a child—an eight-year-old drowned in a pool, a toddler run over in his driveway, the college freshman dead after drinking too much one night, a son lost to suicide. I want to reach out to those mothers and say—say what? Maybe something like, *This article doesn't talk about how you used to cut up his grapes to make sure he wouldn't choke. It doesn't mention how you would stay up all night, cradling her close when she had those high fevers. Remember how you waited by the phone all night, ready to pick him up and bring him home, and the hours you spent praying and desperate, trying to find help? Your baby had a good mother. You are a good mother.*

Protection to me has come to feel like trusting my instincts, doing the best I can, and hoping I am making the right calls. It means knowing that bad things can and will happen and trying not to let that knowledge paralyze me. I know my fears could keep me from letting my kids do the things they need to do to develop and grow.

When our oldest boys were about ten and twelve, we began to notice that they didn't roam. We'd recently moved to a sprawling Florida community that wasn't as easy to navigate as the hometowns Jeffrey and I had lived in growing up or the Virginia city our boys had been comfortable in before our move. And because we hadn't been there long, the kids weren't sure how to find their new friends. But those factors didn't fully explain their lack of exploration. Part of it was due to a shifting culture—most kids our boys knew weren't venturing out either, so it didn't feel natural to ours to set out on their own. But when Jeffrey and I were young, our minds carried within them detailed maps of our communities. We knew where each of our friends lived, could make our way to school and back, and took frequent trips to local stores to run errands for our moms or pick out treats with some pocket money. I learned to steer clear of the mean man who yelled at me for picking flowers, and Jeffrey figured out an alternate route to avoid the neighborhood bullies parked at the end of his block. These were simply things we had to learn to navigate on our own.

Jeffrey was concerned that our boys' lack of roaming could set them back in the long run. By not learning early that they could survive some external stress and experience success on miniventures out into the world, the larger explorations that loomed on their horizons, like driving a car, getting a first job, or going off to college, could seem more anxiety provoking than they needed to be. His long view of parenting says that by not exposing them to small, navigable dangers early, they would be more prone to paralysis later when they ran into bigger, more adult-size troubles. He wanted to make a plan to push the boys out the door.

I had to think that through for a bit. I didn't mind having my kids right there with me at home, safe and close. I worried about the things that could happen to them if we pushed them to freely explore. But I forced myself to dig deeper, to look beyond my immediate fears, and to tune out a twenty-four-hour news cycle confirming that there is always something terrible happening somewhere in the world. The truth was that the crime rates in our community were the same or even lower than when I was a kid, so in theory our boys would be in no more risk than I had been. I also had to face my own potential shame and worry about what other parents would think of me. Would sending our boys out on their own, even occasionally with their youngest brother, be frowned upon? I took a deep breath, and we decided to find out.

Jeffrey went online and pulled up a map of his childhood hometown. He marked out the streets of his youth, figuring out the distance in miles he used to wander when he was young. Next he looked at a map of our new community and measured out a similar distance. He found landmarks and places of interest within that area and took the boys on a bike ride, showing them a little park they could bike to, pointing out friends' houses, and finding a strip mall with a pizza and sandwich shop where they could go to buy a snack.

Finally, he created a few scavenger hunts for them, telling them they had to stick together while hunting for a rare lizard in the green space of a neighborhood next to ours, finding a tucked away playground, and dropping something off for a friend. After they were comfortable with these initial forays out, I took over and started to enjoy the now-old-fashioned role of pushing them out the door. "Go, just go! Go to the pond, or go find someone to play with, but get outside!" Or, "Here's five dollars—go with your brother to get a slice of pizza." I also contributed by making sure they had a flip phone with them on their adventures, more to reassure myself than anything else.

Given my childhood experiences, it's a little odd to even have to write all that out—*Jeffrey's instructions for how to get your kids to leave the house.* But with fear on the rise, it seems increasingly important. Yes, there are dangerous things out there, and trust me, my mind went to all of them. Imagine scrolling news headlines running through my worry-filled brain: *Cars! Alligators! Strangers! Friends with parents with unsecured guns!* But instead of saying no, we taught the boys to watch out for cars and how to turn and signal with their bikes on our sidewalk-less streets. We taught them about stranger danger. We told them to turn and leave immediately if one of their friends started talking about a real gun.

Our calculations would have been different had we been raising brown or black boys in our mainly white, homogeneous Florida neighborhood. We likely would have made a different call. Ultimately, this was one of the reasons why we decided to move our children again when an unexpected opportunity arose for us to travel overseas. We wanted to give the boys the chance to get to know people whose life experiences were very different from their own. We know there is also danger, soul danger, in learning to believe that people who don't look like you should be regarded with fear and suspicion.

But while we were in Florida, I chose to swallow my concerns and believe what Jeffrey told me—that the long-term consequences of teaching our kids that the world is so scary that you can't leave the house are significant. Going out into the world is not risk-free for anyone, especially children. But seeing our boys holed up on the sofa, perfectly safe but not wanting to go out and explore, was an indication to Jeffrey that they were in trouble. To let them go, it helped me to understand there was a risk to our boys' long-term sense of confidence and security if they *didn't* set out into their childhoods and make them their own.

There are of course times when the immediate protection of children is necessary. In these cases, we often act before thinking, as long as we're not paralyzed by stress and fear ourselves. One scorching hot Saturday when our first two boys were little, our family decided to cool off with a trip to the local waterpark. Once there, we discovered that many other people had decided to do the same thing. Jeffrey took Drew to find a spot in the kiddie area while I took Josh to the lazy river. I grabbed a float and entered a mass of humanity being pulled along by a slow current. Lifting my feet and holding on to Josh, I tried to enjoy the coolish water and told myself not to think about germs.

Josh and I bobbed along for a while, bumping uncomfortably into the people pressed around us while we moved through the water. I decided to get out after one loop, and as I put my feet down and tried to pull us to the exit, an angry voice next to me spat the word "Idiot!" into the air. Startled, I looked up in time to see a man with his hand raised, glaring at a boy. My head jerked back involuntarily when the man lowered his hand into a terrible slap.

"Stop bumping into people!" he said loudly while the child, about eight, cowered.

We stepped out of the current, and I sent Josh over to the side of the shallow pool to play. Shaky but determined, I walked over to the man and his boy, who were now standing in the pool as well. It wasn't until I was directly in front of them that I wondered whether I was making a good choice. The muscular, blond man towered over me, but it was too late to go back now. Looking into his eyes, I asked, "Why would you hit a child and call him an idiot for something as silly as bumping into people in a pool? You saw how crowded it was in there! I bumped into people, my son bumped into people, and you probably bumped into people too. You didn't have to hit a kid."

The man looked at me hard before beginning to wiggle his head and speak in a mocking tone, the way some people do when they want to make someone else feel small. "Ooohhh," he said, glowering. "She thinks she knows what I should do with my own kid."

Later, I would wonder about this man's own pain. Who in his life had spoken to him like that, treated him so badly that he had learned to do the same? But right then we just stared at each other for a long moment before I said quietly, "He is a child," and turned to walk away and over to Josh.

As I sat at the side of the pool watching Josh play, I questioned myself. I wasn't sure I should have said anything. I know there's a chance I made it worse. Would the man feel shame at being confronted and take it out on his boy? Very possibly yes. A man who would hurt his son so openly in public was likely to be even harsher in private. But that hard slap in broad daylight had been so blatant and cruel. Other people must have seen it too. Why did no one do anything?

After a while, I noticed that the boy had slowly worked his way over to where Josh was sitting. They played next to each other for a minute, then the boy said something to Josh before paddling away. When Josh returned to me not long after that, I asked him what the boy had said. "It was funny, Mom," Josh replied. "He told me, 'Your mom is my friend.'"

Protecting our own kids is good, necessary, and paramount. But fear can make us push this protection too far, creating fortresses that keep our own children in and leave so many other children out.

Letting go of some of that fear may allow us to be a child's friend. Right now they need all of us, and they especially need *you*, you who care enough that you are sitting here reading a parenting book. So send your kids out into the world, and welcome other kids in too. Get curious about the children who come into your life, especially the hard-to-love ones. Encourage them to knock on your door, and invite them in when they show up, even if it's inconvenient sometimes. If money is tight, feed them with store-brand bread and blocks of cheese and apples, keep driving that old car, and try not to care what your neighbors think. As I've learned from Father Greg Boyle: God is the person in front of you.[1] That counts for kids too.

JEFFREY

A newly crawling baby heads straight for the stairs, a normally easy-going four-year-old cries uncontrollably when left with a certain babysitter, a six-year-old chases a ball into the street, a ten-year-old tells you she feels uncomfortable with the way a family member has approached her, a twelve-year-old asks for a sleepover in a home you believe to be unstable, and a fourteen-year-old begins to hang out with much older, more sophisticated friends.

Protection is one of humanity's most basic needs, and there will be moments in all our kids' journeys when we must draw our children close and stand between them and things that would harm them. On the compass, protection is found in the opposite direction of the safe, relaxed, open-to-possibilities compass point of delight. Protection is vigilant to the reality that there are genuine threats in the world that our children will need our active help navigating.

We also live in a culture that bombards us with constant warnings and reminders about the dangers that could befall our children. And there is no easier way to trigger our natural inclination to protect our kids than to arouse our fears and suspicions about all the bad things that could happen to them or the dangerous people who might want to hurt them. As a parent, you face the challenge of trying to find the balance between too much and too little protection and whether what they are experiencing is a danger to be protected from or simply an obstacle to maneuver. Is the boulder up ahead an exciting challenge that will strengthen and grow your child when she climbs it, or is it more likely to fall over and crush her? You're only going to know the answer to that question if you know your child well enough to have a sense of what is or isn't a true danger on the path she is on.

Protection: What It Is and Why It Matters

When we think of protection, our minds may naturally turn to protecting our kids from accidents, outsiders, and external harms. But from a long-term mental and physical health standpoint, the most urgent dangers our kids as a society face are not the dangers outside our doorsteps but the dangers within; specifically, the dangers of family violence, emotional and physical abuse, and neglect.

A child is significantly more likely to be harmed physically or emotionally by a family member than to be a victim of assault by someone outside his or her family. Around one in five young people report having witnessed violence in their home in their lifetime, and one in four report experiencing caregiver violence, sexual abuse, psychological abuse, neglect, or abduction.[2] A study by the US Department of Justice reports that approximately 30 percent of the perpetrators of childhood sexual abuse are family members, 60 percent are people known to the child, and only 10 percent are strangers.[3] This means that healthy protection of our children often involves complex interpersonal dynamics, which can add to its difficulty. I want to empower you to name and address abuse by understanding the consequences of failing to act when you sense that your child is at risk.

The Effects of Childhood Trauma

A joint research project done by the Center for Disease Control and Prevention (CDC) and the health organization Kaiser Permanente has given us a window of insight into the effects of childhood traumatic events. The project is called the CDC-Kaiser ACE Study, and the CDC tracks over seventeen thousand people who received physical exams and underwent confidential surveys during the mid-1990s.[4] It is one of the largest investigations into the effect of childhood abuse and neglect, and the primary objective of the study is to identify the rates of adverse childhood experiences (ACEs) in people's lives and to determine how those events influence people's physical and mental well-being over time.

In the study, ACEs are defined as including any of the below events in the first eighteen years of a person's life:

- Emotional abuse
- Physical abuse
- Sexual abuse
- Having a mother treated violently
- Having a household member who was a substance abuser
- Having a household member who was mentally ill, depressed, or had attempted suicide
- Having a household member who was incarcerated
- Having parents who separated or divorced
- Emotional neglect
- Physical neglect

These events are classified as adverse childhood experiences because they activate a person's stress-response system, often over long periods of time.

The ACE study reveals that the higher the ACE score a person has, the higher their risk for mental health problems (e.g., depression, anxiety, PTSD), behavioral problems (e.g., drug and alcohol abuse, crime, academic and work failure, etc.), and medical problems (e.g., cardiovascular disease, pulmonary disease, liver problems).[5] Importantly, the risk attributed to early adverse life experiences stands apart from socioeconomic variables that may be associated with having such events, such as poverty. The ACE study suggests that about two in three people have had at least one adverse childhood experience, while one in ten have had more than four such events.[6] The need for protection begins with taking seriously the threat of such experiences to our children and being willing to step between them and unsafe people. And it means educating our children about their rights to be safe, how to identify unsafe people, how to protect themselves, and to always trust their instincts around others, no matter what their title or position.

When we do these things in the context of connection and a secure attachment relationship, we not only protect our children from external harm, we build their resilience. We strengthen them to withstand the worst effects of pain and trauma when it does eventually come into their lives.

What I Most Want You to Know about Protection

Not long ago it was unclear why some people who experience trauma go on to have major mental health problems, including Posttraumatic Stress Disorder (PTSD), while others seem to recover from such events without significant long-term consequences. But when we pair the findings from the ACE study with research from the field of early childhood attachment and trauma, answers begin to emerge. In this area of research, the evidence suggests that having a secure childhood attachment to a primary caregiver creates a protective buffer for people if they experience trauma later in life. The security of a child's early attachments can predict how they will respond to and recover from future traumatic events.[7]

Three central factors put a child at greater risk of
experiencing mental health issues later in life:

- Having certain genetic risk factors[8]
- Having multiple childhood traumatic experiences[9]

- And lacking a secure attachment figure present at the time
  to help them process those traumas[10]

Of these three factors, you have the least control over what genes your child has inherited from you. If you or your spouse, or other blood relatives, have struggled with depression or anxiety, it is very possible that your children could carry risk factors for depression and anxiety. But no one gene determines everything, so it's not inevitable that they will develop those conditions. Having a genetic risk factor simply means that a person is generally more vulnerable to developing certain conditions when exposed to environmental stressors, such as a traumatic event.

Of the other two factors, we've talked about the importance of taking action to protect our children from abuse, neglect, and exposure to violence and trusting our instincts when something doesn't feel right. But even then we will never have total control over what happens to our children. What we do have total control over is the third risk factor: nurturing a secure attachment with our children. When we are open and available to our children when they are in genuine pain, we create pathways in their developing brains for grieving and recovering from pain *with someone*. Having such pathways for processing overwhelming experiences builds resiliency in them against future pain and potential trauma. This matters because life is hard and traumatic life events are a part of the human experience. Children of loving, attentive, and protective parents can still experience trauma. Traumatic accidents, life-threatening health problems, assault, and the loss of loved ones can happen to anyone. Furthermore, one day our children will become adults who set out into the world beyond our limited range of protection. And in that world, they will experience deep, life-altering pain. We all do, eventually.

We cannot protect our children from all pain or alter their genetic risk factors. But we can commit ourselves to fostering secure attachment relationships with our children. Learning to identify and meet your child's six needs more consistently is how you build security in your attachment relationship. Such a relationship is the best immunization you can give your child for the pain they are bound to experience, sooner or later. None of us want to acknowledge that pain is inevitable. We would rather do whatever possible to eliminate all potential pain. But, ultimately, you will not succeed. And the cost of trying to eliminate all sources of pain for your child, rather than focusing on your relationship, may be even more detrimental to them in the long run than trying to protect them from experiencing any pain at all.

The Risk of Overprotection

When we overprotect our children, their threshold for registering potential danger gets lower and lower. So the cost of choosing to protect your child against every potential or simply imagined danger is significant. In essence, we deny our children the opportunity to learn to navigate and master danger themselves. And when our children have no confidence that they can face danger, they become increasingly anxious about the world. Our children avoid more and more, until one day, when it's time for them to walk out the door and make their own way, they don't.

The percentage of children experiencing anxiety has more than doubled since 2003, and we're seeing a growing trend of anxious children and teenagers failing to achieve liftoff to independence in adulthood.[11] Many variables contribute to these increases, and not all children who live at home into adulthood are there because they are afraid of the world. But a significant number of them are. Their frustrated parents bring them into my office regularly. So how you choose to navigate the need for protection will have consequences for your child's future health and functioning in the world.

Finding a Path Forward

If you yourself struggle with anxiety at the thought of sending your child out into the world to try new things and risk life's troubles, it may help to remember that what our children experience in our own homes is the truest indicator of their future health and well-being. Consider again the list of adverse childhood experiences, and ask yourself which of them, if any, may be part of your child's life . Excusing or tolerating family members or acquaintances who engage in any of the ACE behaviors is placing your child at increased risk for lifelong problems across all aspects of his or her lifetime.

Many of us struggle ourselves with depression, anxiety, or the aftereffects of trauma, which can take a toll on the well-being of our children. If you believe your child may be at risk because of your own mental health, then for the sake of your child, you need to prioritize your own needs. Reach out to a therapist or support group, and use the resources we've included in the back of this book and on our website to find a path to help and health.

Many of us also struggle with a family member or partner who is not well and whose presence creates severe stress on the family. If someone is causing your child to experience one or more of the adverse childhood experiences listed above, then, as your child's parent, you may need to prioritize the needs of your child over the needs of someone else you love. Taking such action my feel dangerous because of threats from that person or the power they hold over you, or it may feel excruciatingly painful because of your care and concern for that person. If either is true, please get help from a supportive professional, as well as safe friends and family members. And please do not accept anyone's attempts to dismiss or minimize your situation, no matter their position or title. You and your child are every bit as worthy and valuable as the person who is causing you harm.

The Promise of Faith

In the gospel of John, Jesus tells his disciples the truth: "In this world you will have trouble."[12] But then he goes on to lift up a prayer for them to God: "My prayer is not that you take them out of the world but that you protect them. . . . As you sent me into the world, I have sent them into the world."[13] Rather than asking for his friends to be cloistered away from all trouble, Jesus prays that God will go with them and protect them as they enter the world to transform it with love.

In the midst of this promised trouble, there's another promise we can hold on to. It is the promise of presence, repeated over and over throughout Scripture.

I will not leave you or forsake you . . .

The Lord your God is with you wherever you go . . .

I will strengthen you, I will help you, I will uphold you . . .

Psalm 46:1 reads, "God is our refuge and strength, an ever-present help in trouble."

Allow yourself to be anchored to both promises. There *will* be trouble *and* God will be with you in the midst of that trouble. Love ever-present. Anchoring ourselves and our children in this way allows us to go into the world with confidence, believing that even in pain there is nowhere we can go that is outside the presence of God.

If you can, let yourself enter this same mind-set in your relationship with your children. Our children *will* experience pain because pain is part of life. But we can mitigate this pain by going *with* them and offering healthy protection. When we send them out into the world and they run into trouble, we can meet them where they are and walk with them through their pain to help heal their wounds. When we protect in this way, we strengthen our children to grow in courage and compassion and give them confidence to keep pressing on.

Reality Check

To get a general idea of how responsive you are to the need for protection, look at the following diagram, and consider how prone you are to lean toward one side or the other. Consider asking your parenting partner, a friend, and/or your child to rate you as well. Differences in ratings are opportunities for insight and learning.

Protection

NEED TYPE: TAKING CHARGE

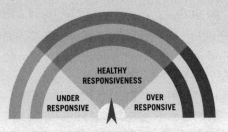

HEALTHY
RESPONSIVENESS

UNDER
RESPONSIVE

OVER
RESPONSIVE

Here are some statements that may feel true if you tend to underrespond to the need for protection:

- I don't feel the need to pay too close attention to where my child is or whom she is with. She knows how to take care of herself.
- If my child wants to do something, I have a hard time saying no, even if the activity or situation makes me uncomfortable.
- If another adult puts my child in his place, he probably had it coming.

Here are some statements that may feel true if you tend to overrespond to the need for protection:

- I never leave my child alone with another adult unless I know that adult really well or have clear assurance of my child's safety.
- I feel very uncomfortable letting my child engage in physical activities or exploration if I think there is any chance he could get hurt.
- I'm not comfortable with letting my child spend too much time away from me with friends, even if I know and like the friends' families.

Small Steps to Take Today

If you feel like you may be undersensitive to your child's need for protection, we have good news. You have likely been giving your child opportunities to discover his own strength and resiliency in the midst of danger and challenges. But we encourage you to explore whether there are relationships or situations that are too dangerous or risky for him to manage on his own without causing potential long-term harm. If this could be the case, consider how you could take steps to protect him.

If you feel like you are oversensitive to your child's need for protection, we have good news for you too. You are communicating to your child that she has value and worth—that she is worth advocating for and protecting. But we encourage you to explore whether her lack of practice navigating danger and difficulty could be robbing her of opportunities to build self-confidence. Consider how you could provide opportunities for her to navigate small risks and obstacles on her own so she can gradually learn how to keep safe when you're not around to protect her.

And what about you? Are you safe now, or are your insides telling you that there is something really wrong, that someone is hurting you or your child in a way that is not right? If that is the case, can you believe *you* are worthy of being loved, defended, and protected? Can you be your own friend? If that's too hard, can you think of someone who can be a friend to you? Can you reach out to that person and hold tight to her hand or let him whisper truth in your ear? It takes a small person to hurt another. Whoever is doing that is pushing their pain onto you, but you don't have to accept it.

If you are in trouble, please believe that you and your kids are worth protecting. We've compiled some resources for you to use at the end of this book in appendixes B and C, some initial stepping-stones to start you on a path toward safety and healing. There can be life and help and so much good for you in the future. We want to help you look ahead with clear eyes and a strong heart and find your way free.

COMFORT: I SEE YOUR SUFFERING

Moving Close to Ease the Pain

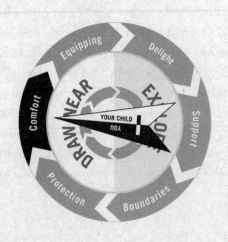

AMY

Hoverboards and Hospital Trips

I never understood the phrase "weak in the knees" until I found myself suddenly kneeling on the floor of my friend Anne's living room, holding Drew's jaggedly broken wrist in my hands. Excited to be visiting dear friends in Asheville, North Carolina, Drew had jumped onto a hoverboard in their kitchen just as their dog ran in front of him. He swerved to miss the dog and fell off the board, completely fracturing his wrist in the process.

It had already been a long few months. An unexpected job opportunity for Jeffrey had opened a door we had dreamed of but never thought possible—the chance to live overseas. One of the former owners of Jeffrey's practice in Florida had moved to take a job in New Zealand, and he introduced Jeffrey to an opportunity there as well. As we weighed the pros and cons of moving to a country we had never even visited, we knew that leaving friends and integrating into a different culture would be especially hard on the older boys. But we didn't see how we could say no. We wanted the boys to know that the world was big, beautiful, and worth exploring, and now we had an opportunity to discover that together. We decided to make the move.

A whirlwind of activity followed—more paperwork than I ever thought possible, packing, and goodbyes. The stress was intense, but we were hoping it would all be worth it. For now, we weren't sure. We had tickets to fly, and all our earthly belongings had already sailed away on a container ship, but our visas for travel had not yet come through. If the visas didn't come, Jeffrey couldn't take the job, and we would be without employment and possessions. While Jeffrey finished up his last week of work in Florida, I traveled with the boys. Jeffrey and I talked on the phone every night, assuring each other that everything would somehow work out. But I'm not sure whether either one of us had fully slept in weeks.

Which brings me back to my position on the floor. Hearing my boy call out, "Mom . . ." and seeing the odd, terrible bend of his wrist had literally crumpled my knees. Now I knelt in front of him, bowing my head for a moment, not in prayer but in panic. The split-second thoughts running through my mind circled around fear, overwhelm, dual-country doctor visits, and sky-high insurance deductibles. I kept my head down for several seconds so I could give myself a pep talk before lifting my head to meet Drew's pain-filled eyes.

Pull yourself together, Amy. This is about Drew and not at all about you. Don't think about anything except what your boy needs right now. There'll be time to work everything else out later. For now, Mom-game on.

Anne ushered us to her car to drive us to the hospital, and I climbed in next to Drew in the middle row of her minivan. Drew has always been unbelievably stoic when it comes to pain, but he moaned in agony every time the car hit a bump. As I sat next to him, trying to keep his arm from jostling, I almost couldn't bear to look at the ache etched on his face. He moaned again as we crossed over railroad tracks, and I felt panic rising up inside me. I was desperate to do something to shut off the hurting.

Glancing down at the floor, I saw, right at my feet, a tiny little plastic hand. Aha! A chance at a joke. Maybe I could make Drew laugh and take his mind off the pain for a bit.

"Buddy," I said, reaching down to pick up the plastic hand from the floor. "Buddy, don't worry. If something goes wrong at the hospital and you end up losing your hand, everything is going to be fine. We already have this one here to replace it!"

Even as I lifted that mini hand into the air, I sensed I was making a mistake. In my desire to ease my own discomfort at seeing Drew in so much pain, I had terrified him. "Mom!" he screamed. Then, for the first time since the accident, he started to cry.

"Oh, honey, I'm so sorry. That was just a bad joke. Of course you won't lose your hand. I was just trying to make you laugh." In the rearview mirror, I caught Anne's eye and saw her shaking her head at me, trying not to laugh at my nonsense herself.

Anne then voiced a much more appropriate response to his misery. "We'll be there soon to get your wrist taken care of, Drew. Hang in there. I'm sorry it hurts so much."

We did get Drew's wrist taken care of at the hospital, but the doctor warned that even with pain medication, Drew had a very uncomfortable night ahead of him. Nathan and I were sleeping in the basement of our friends' home that week, so I decided that it would be best if Drew joined us there as well, just in case his pain became unmanageable.

At about one o'clock in the morning, the pain woke him up. He moaned every time he moved, and making him even more miserable was the fact that his nose was running nonstop. He asked for tissues, and I handed him all I could find—a roll of toilet paper. We sat next to each other on the bed for a very long time—Drew in awful discomfort, ripping off pieces of toilet paper and blowing his dripping nose with his one good arm, me sitting paralyzed next to him, occasionally rubbing his back. Exhausted, I was hardly able to think, much less do anything to help.

A little after three in the morning, our noise and the light from a lamp woke up six-year-old Nathan, who climbed up from his mattress on the floor to join us on the bed. He quietly assessed the situation—Drew's tears, his running nose, and the effort it was taking him to rip off pieces of toilet paper. Wordlessly, he reached over to Drew and took the paper from his hand, then started ripping off pieces of the roll for Drew to use the next time he needed to blow his nose. Turning to me, Nathan said in a loud whisper, "Mom, I'm trying to do something that will help Drew. What are *you* doing to help Drew right now?"

I reached out my hand and took over the toilet paper ripping.

Someone recently asked Jeffrey which need he thought was most important. His response surprised me. "Comfort," he responded.

"I think it's comfort." He believes that comfort is the need people find most personally painful and difficult to understand, so it's often skipped over or rushed through. He believes we're living in a world that hasn't learned to make space for comfort, and because of this, comfort's importance has become paramount.

I've been turning his words over in my mind ever since, and they're beginning to make more sense to me. Jeffrey has always said he feels his greatest honor and biggest role as a therapist is to bear witness. He works with people to explore places where they are stuck and to find a path forward, of course. But to do this, he must first open himself up to be a vessel for their pain. He listens to give people a safe space to unload some of the heavy weight they are carrying. And by simply recognizing and acknowledging the pain of their experience, he is able to take on some of that heaviness himself. This can lighten the load enough to help someone shift out of grief or reactivity and begin to move forward again.

People in pain can be crushed by their experiences. They can close themselves off or scream pain out loud in any way they can until everyone is forced to hear. It can be hard to be close to them. But what if instead of turning away, denying their experience or trying to rush them through it, we made room for comfort? What if we drew close together through the dark, painful nights, whatever those nights may be?

I will never fully understand the depth of someone else's pain any more than I could feel the sharp dagger stab of Drew's jagged wrist. But I can mourn with those who mourn. I can weep. And I'm learning to let myself feel the weight of the moment before looking to find a quick way to push forward again.

Nathan's quiet ripping of the toilet paper for our suffering Drew was a reminder that I don't have to do anything extraordinary to provide comfort. Surrendering to the fact that I can't fix everything allows me to find small ways to simply be present. And even though I wasn't a perfect comforter that night with Drew, I was still right there with him, which in the end is what matters. When I asked him later what he remembered about the experience, he told me that he remembered me. He remembered how I had been close to him that day and all through the long night. He said it made him feel like everything would be okay, except for one thing.

"That joke, Mom. That joke about the hand. That joke was *really* bad."

JEFFREY

A two-year-old screams with terror after getting barked at by a dog behind a fence. A four-year-old takes a hard tumble and scrapes her knee. A six-year-old mourns the loss of his pet fish, and an eight-year-old doesn't get invited to a friend's birthday party. An eleven-year-old cries after her father moves out, a thirteen-year-old isn't chosen for a school play, and a fifteen-year-old loses a friend in a car accident.

Our children are going to experience pain, and comfort is how we enter into that pain, even when it's hard to relate to or painful for us to deal with too.

Comfort: What It Is and Why It Matters

The Merriam-Webster definition of *comfort* is "to give strength and hope to" and derives from the Latin root *fortare*, as in *fortitude*. Merriam-Webster also defines *comfort* as "to ease the grief or trouble of." When we comfort, we are both easing pain and strengthening our children. We join their suffering and provide refuge through their emotional storm until the way clears enough to find a path forward again. Sometimes the storm passes in a flash, but other times the storm feels unending, so comfort often requires patience, kindness, and emotional strength on our part too.

Of all the needs on the compass, comfort is perhaps the most complicated and challenging to understand and grapple with.

Because comfort requires sharing in our children's pain, it is almost always *un*comfortable for us. Loving parents do not want to see their children in pain, so when we understand their pain, we want to somehow make it go away, both for our children's sake *and* for ours. And sometimes we have trouble understanding our children's pain. It may not make sense to us, or it might seem frivolous and overstated based on what we can observe. In either case, we can be tempted to rush our children to move on and quickly past it. But the research is clear that providing our children with comfort is essential to their future functioning, and how a parent navigates comfort strongly shapes how a child will be able to navigate their own emotional life as they mature into an adult.[1]

Protection and comfort can work together with a pursuing, incarnational love. Picture a Coast Guard helicopter hovering over a drowning man thrashing in the waves. Imagine that a storm had been predicted and the man made a foolish decision to venture out in his boat—he is now suffering the consequences of his poor choice. Does the Coast Guard rescuer open the door of the helicopter and yell down advice or criticism to the drowning man? Or, slightly better, does the rescuer simply throw down a rope and hope the man will be able to catch it? No, the rescuer must tie the rope around his waist and lower himself down into the crashing waves. He puts himself in harm's way so that he can grab the drowning man and pull him to safety. There may be a time for advice or correction later, but the first priority is to use strength and wisdom to calm and secure the person and retreat with them to a place of warmth and safety.

Many parents believe that if they overindulge in comfort with their children, their kids will be dependent on comfort from others when they are older. The truth is quite the opposite! Giving generous attention to our children's need for comfort will enable them, as they mature, to learn to comfort themselves in healthy ways. Put another way, providing healthy comfort increases the chance that your child will be less emotionally needy and vulnerable to emotional storms as an adult, as well as less likely to engage in destructive forms of self-comfort. Rather than weakening them, giving comfort generously *strengthens* our children.

Children with secure attachment relationships are children who are regularly comforted growing up. The experience of having difficult emotions calmed by a loving caregiver trains these children's nervous systems how to regulate and calm themselves. Receiving comfort also teaches children how to give comfort to others and to understand that it is reasonable to expect comfort from others when they are in need. This pushes them into relationships with people who can also give and receive comfort well. These secure children tend to seek out relationships with other secure children. They tend to avoid children, and eventually romantic partners, who are less emotionally resilient.[2] So, when we meet the need for comfort in our children, we equip them to regulate difficult emotions on their own, while also making it more likely for them to be in relationship with emotionally supportive people in times of need. It's a double win.

What I Most Want You to Know about Comfort

In the chapter on boundaries, we introduced the idea that you and your child have two different brain systems that direct your behavior: the feeling, or emotional, brain and the thinking brain. In an ideal world, we are able to operate out of both brain systems simultaneously, with our feeling brain providing motivation and energy and our thinking brain providing structure, planning, and direction.

Depending on temperament and circumstances, sometimes we adults may tip to the feeling side of the scale, and at other times we may tip to the rational, thinking side. But if we know ourselves well, balance can be relatively easily restored. If I get too stuck in my head, overthinking or ruminating about things, I might consciously engage in some emotionally enjoyable activity

to get unstuck and back in balance. Or if I get stuck in a negative emotional state, I might consciously engage in some rational
reappraisals of my situation (e.g., "This too shall pass," "Everybody
makes mistakes sometimes," "I know I'm still loved," etc.) to help
me get back in balance.

But even as adults it is difficult to live with such balance, especially if things are hard or we're under stress. And because of the way
their brains are developing, it's often impossible for our children.
Remember that a child's information-processing scale is naturally
weighted to the feeling side of their brain, like this:

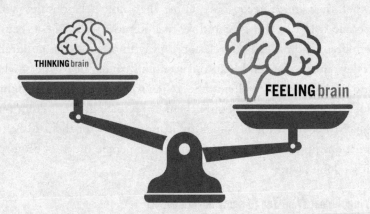

THINKING brain

FEELING brain

Because of this early imbalance, a young child tends to get easily weighed down in his emotions. As children grow older, their
reasoning capacity grows, as does their ability to use their thoughts
to help them work through emotionally stressful events. Whereas
the three-year-old who is told she can't have a cookie may have a
full-on temper tantrum that no manner of reason can quell, you
can probably explain the situation to your nine-year-old ("We are
saving the cookies for when people come over tonight") and can
offer a plan ("But we'll make sure you get one after dinner"). Doing
this may avert the tantrum because your nine-year-old has capacity
for reasoning on the thinking side of his brain that your three-year-
old does not.

The Importance of Presence and Mirroring

When confronted with their child's distress, most parents try to push down on the rational-thinking side of their child's brain-processing scale to avert a complete emotional "takeover." And often that works. Indeed, this is key to the strategies that fall under support and boundaries, when parents anticipate and respond to emerging stressors that their child is facing. Reasoning and explanations before an anticipated stressor help children navigate obstacles in front of them without falling apart.

But what happens when that *doesn't* work? When the tears, the anger, or the anxiety comes out in full force? When your child's brain scale is overloaded with emotion and looks more like this?

Some parents intuitively know to move away from explanations and rationalizations and move toward the language of the feeling brain, using things like tone, touch, and facial expression to reach their children. They join in their child's distress in a manner that doesn't resist it outright but rather sits alongside the suffering without pressure or impatience. They lower their voice and say, "Oh, honey come here." They pull their child in to be held or hold her hand. They say, "Tell me more about what's going on" and ask other questions that help draw out the often-hidden particulars of the pain their child is carrying. They value their child's emotional experience enough to see and name it through their child's eyes as best they can—like a mirror—and offer hypotheses that their child can correct or build upon. They say things like, "It looks like you're really disappointed. Is that what's going on? I get that. I think I would be disappointed too." Or, "I see it's really scary for you. Are you afraid of what's going to happen when you get to school?" They allow for silence when there aren't any words to say, or the words can't be found, and just sit beside their child while the waves of pain pass over.

Through their presence, and by not trying to convince their child of anything or to fix the problem and force the pain away, these parents lessen the weight of the pain their child is carrying. They lighten the load of their child's emotional experience, which makes their child more open to processing what is going on using their rational, thinking brain. And only when the scale becomes more balanced can the thinking part of their child's brain be acted on in a productive manner.

Every parent needs to know that if your child is in a scales-fully-tipped-to-the-feeling-side-of-their-brain position, no manner of words, no matter how well or loudly said, are going to make the situation better. Your wisdom and insight are literally inaccessible to your child's rational, thinking brain in that position. You are wasting your breath, and likely to only make things worse.

So why do we talk louder and harder when it's clear that our children are stuck in their emotions? More often than not, it's because the scales have tipped to the emotional side in our own brains, too. We are upset and are trying to get *ourselves* back into balance by winning an argument or talking and rationalizing our way back to calm. And when that doesn't work, we double down. We want to make our child see things with a rational adult brain. But they cannot. Because they are neither rational in that moment, nor do they have an adult brain to see things as an adult can see them. So, in storms of emotions, our children need us to sit with their emotions and mirror back to them what we see, reflecting *their* point of view. That is what will ease their pain and help the storm to pass so that they can think again and move forward.

The Powerful Pull of Comfort

Attachment research shows that we are hardwired to respond to our children's pain, and our children are hardwired to seek comfort from us when they experience pain. This means that the expression of pain holds particular power in your relationship. So in some relationships, your child's expression of pain is their ace in the hole for your attention because you cannot resist responding to it, either through concerned care or frustrated reactivity. Because of this power of pain, we parents can easily fall into the trap of questioning the authenticity of our children's expressions of pain. We become suspicious that our children are "manipulating" us with their emotions. At one point or another, most parents will question whether their comforting is doing more harm than good. We ask ourselves, "Am I just getting played?" or accuse our spouse that, "She has you wrapped around her finger with her tears."

Two Situations When Comfort May Not Be Helpful

Two types of emotional storms are worth considering more carefully in this regard. The first case is the storm of frustrated will, also known as the pain of discovering that, in the immortal words of Mick Jagger, "You can't always get what you want." Human beings are an adamant bunch. We want what we want, how we want it, and when we want it. You do. I do. And your kid surely does. As you meet your child's needs for boundaries by saying no to them, there will be much wailing and gnashing of teeth from time to time. Give your child the gift of learning that they can get through the pain of not getting everything they want. Let them weep, let them gnash, and respect their process of grieving that they can't always have it their way. Try not to jump in to save them or, conversely, shame them for their wants and desires. Try to ignore the outcries of unfairness as much as possible, and don't feed the flame. Just let them have their moment, and meet them on the other side once the storm has passed.

The other kind of situation that may not respond well to comfort is when a child is trying on their emotions for effect or out of habit rather than out of spontaneous pain or turmoil. Discerning this can be tricky business, but the beauty of the compass is that the worst thing that can happen is that you have misread the situation and you switch course once you realize that the direction you thought you needed to go was in fact an unhelpful one. When comfort does not seem to help, switch course, usually by either setting boundaries or simply taking a time-out from the situation. Sometimes giving time and space is the most productive action two people stuck in an emotional storm can take to get back to a place where they can move forward together again. Know also that if your child seems to be struggling frequently and coming to you with what feels like exaggerated pain and requests for comfort, he may need more positive attention from you generally. Could it be that using the powerful pull to comfort is the only way he feels he can get you to offer your affection and love? If it feels like that could be true for your child, try turning to the other emotional compass point of delight in the moments when your child is not struggling or in pain. A weepy, clingy, or cranky child may truly need consistent, attentive, and affectionate care in times without pain.

Gender and Comfort

The data is clear that parents treat their boys and girls differently when it comes to displays of distress.[3] Boys are socialized that vulnerable expressions of pain are generally not acceptable unless they come in the form of aggression, which is considered "natural."

Consciously or unconsciously, society considers it a disservice to boys to help them feel and understand their fears and their tears, believing boys need to be tough to survive. But choosing that path for them robs them of empathy, connection, and the possibility of emotional mastery. This kind of thinking leads to boys who become men who only know the language of raw anger for their pain and who are only allowed to find comfort in male-sanctioned outlets like sex, aggression, and thrill-seeking.

Conversely, girls are socialized to believe that vulnerable expressions of pain are appropriate and valid but aggression is not. Society considers it a disservice to girls to help them feel and understand their anger and gives girls a message that their anger is anything from unladylike and unattractive to overbearing and offensive. This leads to girls becoming women who only know the language of helplessness for their pain and who feel uncomfortable exercising inner power and strength to overcome difficult experiences. This has huge cross-generational and societal implications.

As you parent, remember that comfort is a universal human need. Ask yourself whether you would be providing the same type of comfort to your child if they were a different gender, and if not, wonder why. Are fear or societal expectations driving your reactions more than knowledge about who your children are and how they might benefit from your wholehearted willingness to enter into their pain? If so, could you try to put those fears and expectations aside and respond with the form of comfort they seem to genuinely need?

A Model of Entering into Pain

The shortest sentence in the Bible is "Jesus wept." In my mind, it is also one of the most beautiful and important. Jesus had been called to come tend to his close friend Lazarus, who was gravely ill. When Jesus heard of the illness, he said, "This sickness will not end in death,"[4] but when he arrived at Lazarus's home, Lazarus's sisters, Mary and Martha, were mourning their brother's death. There at this scene of great sadness and pain, Jesus joined his tears with his friends'. Jesus wept.

The account makes it clear that Jesus knows the story will end with his friend alive and well, even though no one believes him. The gospels tell us that after entering into their pain with them, Jesus went to Lazarus's tomb and called out to God and to his friend. "Lazarus, come out!"[5] And Lazarus walked out of his grave, fully alive.

My faith gives me hope that, despite all I can see, one day there will be a time when perfect peace, or shalom, will reign— when all our tears will be wiped away. I certainly don't know exactly when or how that will happen, but I draw strength from the promise of it and accept the invitation to express that peace in my own life, as best I am able. In the meantime, I fully expect life to be painful and commit to entering into the pain of my children and my fellow human beings, giving comfort as I can. I'm strengthened by knowing that Jesus himself did not transcend pain. Faced with the death of Lazarus and the grieving of his friends, he joined his emotional life with theirs. He didn't skip over the pain and go straight to the solution. The comfort Jesus brought to their pain did not begin with fixing their problem but with joining it. He wept *with* them.

Reality Check

To get a general idea of how responsive you are to the need for comfort, look at the following diagram, and consider how prone you are to lean toward one side or the other. Consider asking your parenting partner, a friend, and/or your child to rate you as well. Differences in ratings are opportunities for insight and learning.

Comfort

NEED TYPE: MIRRORING

Here are some statements that may feel true if you tend to underrespond to the need for comfort:

- My first instinct is to assure my child that he is all right unless he's clearly hurt badly.
- I find it uncomfortable to linger in a hug with my child, to hold hands, or to otherwise engage in extended acts of affection.
- I tend to distract myself when I am upset about something, and I do the same for my child if they are upset.

Here are some statements that may feel true if you tend to overrespond to the need for comfort:

- I feel the need to touch, hold, and soothe my child at the first signs of distress or discomfort, whether or not he asks for it.
- I have trouble letting my child move away from me if I am unsure whether the hurt she is carrying is truly gone.
- I always try to make my child talk to me about what is going on inside her if she looks upset or doesn't seem like her normal self.

Small Steps to Take Today

If providing comfort is hard for you, the next time your child is struggling, instead of trying to shut off their emotions, allow yourself to be present. Focus on your own breath for several seconds and tell yourself that this too shall pass, no matter how intense it seems. Remember that a child's life is emotionally stormy because his brain hasn't yet formed the capacity to see the big picture. While what you may want him to learn or do is important, remind yourself that he won't be able to move forward until his storm has passed. Stay calm and bear witness to the big feeling he's having, showing him you'll be there with him through his pain.

Or maybe you're really comfortable with comfort, so comfortable that you tend to jump right in to hold and soothe and reassure at the slightest indication of pain, fear, or disappointment your child might be feeling. If this is the case, consider that jumping in too quickly to offer comfort can prime a child to expect pain and distress, even when it's not truly warranted. Offering comfort right away, especially when it's not solicited, robs your child of the opportunity to find comfort within herself. So if you lean toward overresponding to the need for comfort, watch and wait. Instead of moving to comfort immediately, pause and ask your child whether she needs help with her emotions, then be willing to respect her desire to find her own way. Let her fall down and pick herself up sometimes. And know that she still needs you and is connected to you, even as she learns to find comfort and strength on her own.

EQUIPPING: WHERE TO FROM HERE?

Finding a Way Forward with Hope and a Plan

AMY

Pterogators and After-Dinner Walks

When the boys were little, I tried to guide and inspire them by saying things like "Remember who you are" and "You are kind. You are brave. You are strong." My hope was that these statements would empower them and that my words would seep into their consciousness to become part of their identity.

Nathan is the child who officially broke me of this process. An independent thinker practically from birth, he had no use for my imposed definitions. When he was three, I tried to point him to better behavior by telling him: "Nathan, don't crumple up Drew's paper. You are a kind boy, and kind boys share paper."

Nathan looked at me for a long moment before declaring, "I *not* a kind one. I a *mean* one!" Then, for the next few months, he would walk around the house at odd times, swinging a toy sword and saying, "I *is* a mean one. I is a *widy* mean one."

Sigh.

I think Nathan's self-assurance was a gift because it made me realize that the statements I was making to my boys were actually prayers rather than truth based on knowledge of who they were. They were things I had to take up with God—*"Let them be brave, let them be kind. In moments when they feel alone, let them remember who they belong to."* The only true and absolute statement I could speak over all of them was simple and undeniable. They are loved. If I wanted to say anything else about them, I needed to know them. And to do that, I had to make space for them to tell me who they believe themselves to be.

My boys don't typically open up to simple questions. Asking, "How was your day?" or "Who did you play with today at school?" is often met with a one-word answer or nondescript response. As I sought out ways to reach them, a friend of mine told me that taking walks with her now-grown boys had been a meaningful way to connect with them. And then, in the middle of a time when Josh seemed particularly reluctant to share much with us, I read an article about how sustaining eye contact can feel shameful or threatening to men and boys[1] and that walking side by side may open up pathways to connection. I decided to give it a try, and one summer evening when Josh was about nine, I invited him to come on a walk with me.

Within fifteen seconds of our feet hitting the pavement, my boy started to talk. He continued talking for about forty-five minutes about a very specific topic, or rather, a very specific book, a book called *Killer Species: Menace from the Deep*. Subject: The Pterogator, a mutant mix of alligator and owl, a ferocious species created to unleash havoc on the pythons in Florida's Everglades.

At first I waited for this particular train of conversation to end. I wanted to talk about something real and important. But, of course, this topic *was* real and important to Josh. It mattered to him that I was there with him, and he was excited that I was listening. As we slowly approached the house at the end of that first long walk, Josh paused and said, "Mom, what if . . . what if we put a tent over our yard and put an Indo-Pacific gecko in there? They don't need a female to mate, and we could come back months later, and there would be *hundreds* of them!"

What if, my friend? What if, indeed.

Over time, after-dinner walks with the boys have become a ritual. We'll have stretches where we walk almost every night, then breaks where we only walk occasionally. I've learned that if one of the boys asks me to walk, it's usually because he needs some attention or has something on his mind that he wants help working out. Talking through things does seem easier when we're moving side-by-side. It provides a safe place for us to work out what they're going through together.

After our last move, we mapped out a new walking trail. Our New Zealand visas had eventually come through, just days before we were scheduled to depart. As we settled in our new home, we marked out a path that looped around neighborhood streets and behind a primary school, then down through a wooded ravine behind our house. But it had been a while since our last walk when Jeffrey uncovered a lie one of the boys was telling us. Our boy was hiding behaviors and telling calculated untruths so that he could play an online video game, well past the limits we'd given him for game playing. This behavior caught me off guard. It wasn't exactly his actions that upset me—that part just made me feel worried. But when I thought about the deliberate way he'd behaved, the things he'd made up and said to me, and the nonchalant way he'd pulled it off, I felt hurt, angry, and disappointed.

Jeffrey sat down with our boy to tell him he'd been discovered and to swap out his laptop for a simpler tablet, one adequate for meeting his school's device requirements but unable to play games. He told him that he could get his computer back when he showed us that he was ready for it—when he'd learned to ask for what he wanted and articulate why it was important to him. He also told him that the most important thing he needed to do was to repair his relationship with us, to show us that he wanted to regain our broken trust.

The next time I saw my boy, he wouldn't look at me. He whispered, "I'm sorry, Mom," but wouldn't say any more than that. We settled into a new normal, relating to each other on a surface level while he remained withdrawn and angry. I prayed for wisdom to know how to reach him. One afternoon while he was at school, my eyes lingered on a photograph taken of the boys when they were little. Bright smiles beamed up from the photo, and as I traced my boy's face I felt tears beginning to form. *Is this it?* I wondered. *Is there some inevitable part of growing up that's going to kick in now? Where children and parents exist in conflict, at odds with each other?* Beyond my hurt and anger, there was fear. Had I lost my son?

Jeffrey decided to take him camping the following weekend. It would be good for them to reconnect and get out in nature—to stare up at the stars and drink in the beauty and to consider their place in this vast universe for a while. Instead of quieting my mind while they were gone, I filled a mindless hour scrolling through my

Facebook feed. A meme shared by a friend made me pause. It said something like, *In our family, we make up secret handshakes and dance around the dinner table and create our own games so that our children will always know they belong.* Studying it, I felt a wave of grief hit me. I wanted a family like that too. But I quickly covered my grief with a blanket of snark. *Well, bully for you and your perfect little happy-clappy, secret-handshaking family,* I thought, then continued to scroll.

But I couldn't shake the dark feelings that the meme had brought on. Later, and away from my phone, I stopped to think them through. I know myself well enough to understand that when my pain has turned into bitterness or disdain, it's an indication that I've gotten offtrack. I tried to remember what I know. Growth trust asks us to believe that our children are always learning and growing—that they are constantly reorganizing what they've learned in the process of becoming who they are meant to be. Just because we can't see that growth in the moment doesn't mean it's not happening. I also know that as kids grow up, they sometimes have to push their parents away so they can find their own way. Separating from us can be a good, necessary part of development. I needed to rise above my hurt and anger and get curious so I could help my son separate in ways that were healthy, not harmful.

That night, home from the camping trip, my boy retreated into his room again. I knocked on his door, and he opened it looking down, still unable to meet my eyes. "Hey, bud," I asked. "Want to go for a walk?"

He shrugged and nodded. "Yeah. I guess so. If you do."

We bundled up against the winter air and headed into the night, walking together in silence down the dark driveway. As we turned onto the street, I asked him how he was doing. He said quietly, "Mom, I feel so ashamed. I just feel so much shame right now. I'm sorry I hurt you. I don't know how to get over this."

I told him that I had been hurt and angry when I found out what he had done, and I was still confused by his actions. But more than anything, I loved him and would always be there for him, no matter what. We couldn't let shame have a place in our relationship because shame would build a wall between us. Shame can make people who love each other go to war. I wanted us to put shame aside and get through this mistake together by figuring out what we could learn from it. Understanding what was going on would help us love each other better, and learning to navigate these hard feelings would be important for his future relationships too.

I asked him to share what was going on inside him. Was something hurting him right now? He must be experiencing some pretty hard things if he was willing to lie and risk our relationship like he had. What was upsetting him, causing him pain? I wanted to hear all of it, even if the people causing his pain were his dad and me. I asked him please not to worry about me or my feelings. I needed to know about him.

At first he didn't seem to understand. "What do you mean, tell you about my pain, Mom?"

I said, "Well, you know what cutting is, right?" He nodded. "Well, why do people cut?"

"Because they would rather feel physical pain than emotional pain."

"Yes. It's a form of numbing. And how do you think *you* numb, or stop yourself from feeling painful things?"

His voice grew soft. "Video games."

"Yeah. I see you numbing through video games. And now you've even done things that seem really unlike you, like lying to Dad and me, so that you can keep playing. That's why I want to know about your pain. What is hurting you, honey? What are you trying not to feel?"

They started to spill out then, the things he'd been carrying alone. He shared about how much he missed his friends in Florida. He spent a lot of time thinking about how they would grow up and move on and forget about him. There was so much pain in his voice when he spoke that truth aloud, so we walked on in silence for a bit after he shared, holding the pain together. As we continued on, I learned more. Some of the things he shared were so poignantly universal to growing up that they made my heart ache. We didn't solve any problems while we walked, but I got to listen, and he got to see that I was still there for him and hear that I had felt a lot of the same things when I was his age.

As we rounded the corner toward home, I asked him to keep talking, to not let shame get in the way and to get Jeffrey and me to help him if he needed it or to tell us if he wanted to talk to a counselor or consider changing schools. We were here for him, and we were going to keep encouraging him to find healthy ways to face his pain head-on. We hugged before going back inside, arms wrapped around each other, fastening our hearts back together again.

I hope you and your kids have many moments of joy and dancing around the dinner table together. I promise not to begrudge you your secret handshakes. But I also want you to know that you're not alone if some days are hard and you are angry or scared or disappointed when you don't know how to help your kid. There is rough terrain on all our journeys, and conflict and heartache that will never show up on any curated social media feed. Let's choose to believe that this breaking and healing, pulling apart and coming back together again, is a natural, even necessary, part of our kids' development.

So now I lift a new prayer to the One who protects, the One who comforts, the One who equips:

Oh God who sees us, dear Counselor and Friend—thank you for your promise of presence. Be near. Pull us close, and go with my children to the places I cannot. Stay with them and guide their way. When the pain is too great or the path feels too hard, bring us back together. Remind them, please, that they never walk alone.

JEFFREY

A one-year-old creeps close to the stairs, then backs away, hesitant after taking a fall. A three-year-old eyes the oven, holding the bandaged finger she's burned after touching the stovetop. A six-year-old doesn't want to go to school because his playmates exclude him on the playground. An eight-year-old feels stress over her teacher's harsh tone of voice. An eleven-year-old is punished at camp for being in a fight, a thirteen-year-old has her phone taken away after chatting with a stranger, and a sixteen-year-old has been dumped by his first serious girlfriend.

Equipping: What It Is and Why It Matters

Our kids are going to make mistakes. They're going to have difficult encounters in the world and with others. Equipping is how we help them make sense of these difficult or confusing experiences and chart a path forward after life's inevitable conflicts and setbacks. If comfort is drawing near to your child and providing refuge in the midst of emotional storms, then equipping can be thought of as the process of assessing the situation once the worst of the storm is over. Equipping is how we help our children understand their difficult experiences so they can move forward feeling prepared and hopeful about facing similar experiences in the future.

As with support and boundaries, comfort and equipping are closely linked to each other. Comfort without equipping may settle our children, but it won't prepare them for the next encounter with similar circumstances. Equipping without comfort tends to result in empty words that our children reject outright, or fail to integrate and make use of, because lingering emotional pain gets in the way of fully processing what we have offered them. Studying for a test when you are having an emotional meltdown tends to be wasted time. The information just doesn't stick. The same is true for equipping conversations that happen without comfort, because comfort is needed first.

In psychological terms, the need for equipping is the need we all have to make sense of our emotionally difficult and troubling experiences. And making sense of things is not easy, especially when you are a child. First there are our emotions, which can be complex and not obvious to others based on how we may be acting. A preschooler who is lashing out for being called a baby does not look like he is embarrassed. A sibling telling her brother that his drawing is stupid does not look like she's jealous. A third grader ignoring requests to put his shoes on for school does not look like he's scared of facing the bully in his classroom. Second, there are our thoughts, which feed and fuel our emotions but which can be irrational or misinformed. Then there are the thoughts and emotions of people around us, which drive how they behave toward us. Finally, there is the question of "What do I do?" None of this information is written clearly on a board for all to see and agree on.

Understanding our own inner life and the inner lives of others is an essential skill that develops over time and takes conscious effort to cultivate. Attending to this skill is especially important in a world that is increasingly experienced at a distance, through technology. In our kids' online lives, it's becoming harder to discern what is true and real and to work through difficult and uncomfortable things. Missing out on the practice of working through pain and misunderstanding face-to-face in interpersonal relationships can make the prospect of facing real live people seem confusing and overwhelming and worth avoiding, if you can.[2] There is good reason to believe that the rise of virtual human interactions over face-to-face interactions is at least partially to blame for the sudden rise in rates of clinical anxiety in children over the past decade, coinciding with the introduction and quick assimilation of smartphones in modern society.[3]

What I Most Want You to Know about Equipping

The practice of moving past storms *together* helps our children understand how their own minds work, read others more accurately, and make wiser life choices.[4] When we embrace the need for equipping in our children, we strengthen them. But what exactly does equipping look like?

A Three-Step Process of Equipping

Step 1: Emotions. Naming emotions helps children make sense of painful experiences. You name emotions when you say things like, "I know you say you're mad because your sister is sitting in your favorite chair. Do you think you might also be a little jealous that she gets to go to a birthday party today and you don't? I used to feel jealous when my sister got to go somewhere without me." Or "I hear you say you hit your brother because he is stupid. But I wonder whether you felt left out because he didn't want to play with you today. I noticed him shutting the door on you a lot. I remember feeling left out by my older sister when I was your age."

As long as you have a sensitive understanding of the situation and aren't insisting that you know *exactly* how they feel, naming emotions can help your child feel less alone. It can be comforting for a child to hear, "I think I know that feeling. I experience it too sometimes." Naming emotions is equipping because naming something is often the first step toward feeling some sense of control over it. Conversely, feeling alone and confused is rarely comforting or productive.

Some parents will get stuck on the idea that naming someone else's experience for them is impossible and perhaps even unethical. But you can't learn to name your own experience if you don't first have a language for it, and a person cannot spontaneously develop a language for his inner experience any more easily than a person can spontaneously learn to solve a math problem. Our children depend on the people around them to develop understanding of their emotions. Saying "I wonder whether you are feeling . . ." or "It looks like you may be feeling . . ." or "I think you may be feeling . . ." are ways to have a conversation while still respecting your child's autonomy.

Other parents will get stuck with naming emotions because they themselves struggle to find language for their own emotions. You can't teach a language you yourself don't speak very well! This is often the case for men, who are discouraged from naming and exploring their emotional lives from an early age, but women struggle with having language for their emotional experience too. Early attachment experiences for both boys and girls play an essential role in how comfortable a person is with exploring their emotional life as an adult.

The good news is that developing a working language for emotions is much easier than learning a foreign language. Think of it more like learning a color wheel. There are primary emotions, just like there are primary colors. Most of the more nuanced emotions are just blends of those primary emotions. You don't need to be able to identify and describe the difference between fuchsia and lavender to be able to help your child with her different emotional shades. An emotion word is just a label for a certain kind of experience of the world. What matters most is developing a language that helps you and your child understand his experience, not whether or not a word is being used "just right." Spend time with this chart, and reflect on various emotions and the situations in your life when you may have experienced those feelings. Then use those memories to guide you in helping your child create her own color wheel of emotions. And don't forget that sometimes your child's big emotions are really just signs of being tired, hungry, sick, in pain, or over-stimulated.

Physical feelings that drive emotions include: *Tired, Hungry, Sick, In Pain, Overstimulated*

Step 2: Thoughts. Our feelings always have thoughts attached, and the next key component of equipping is to help your child understand the thoughts that go with the feelings she is having. Sometimes those thoughts are obvious because your child is announcing them loud and clear. *You hate me! I hate you! I'll never be able to do it! My teacher thinks I'm stupid. All the kids were laughing at me. Nobody wants to be my friend.*

When our children make their thoughts known like this, we are often tempted to jump in and correct them. *That's not true! You don't mean that! Your teacher loves you! I'm sure not everyone was laughing at you. What about Jamie, she's your friend.* Resist this temptation. In those moments, our children are not looking for arguments from us; they're looking for comfort. View these kinds of heated statements as invitations to name feelings first. *You feel like I don't love you? You feel really angry at me? You feel like giving up? You feel like you let your teacher down? You felt embarrassed in front of everyone? You feel like nobody wants to be your friend anymore?*

But once the intensity of an experience dies down, it is important to help your child understand his thoughts. Because our rawest emotions will often tell us lies, if we don't question them, we can carry those lies forward with us even after the intensity of the moment has passed. Exploring your child's thoughts with him after an emotional storm has passed will help both of you figure out what is true about what he is telling himself. It is worth pushing back on potential distortions to help your child see the more complete picture.

After the storm begins to calm, it is time to ask, "Do you really think . . . ?" It's also the time to wonder with your child about other things he tells himself that may be part of the problem. Try to unearth any fears or misunderstanding about something that has happened, or will happen, and about what others may be thinking or feeling. Just as with emotions, your child may need your help understanding their thoughts, and it's okay to throw out guesses.

Did you think I was mad at you? Did you think we weren't ever going to be able to come back? Did you think something bad was going to happen?

If your child holds on to thoughts that you believe are untrue, or at least incomplete, try not to get offended or irritated. Sadly, the human mind is very biased toward information that confirms our emotional hunches. If it feels true, we look for evidence to prove that it is true and resist evidence to the contrary, especially when we feel strongly about something.

Arguably the best long-term strategy to help our children expand their thinking is not to insist on a different conclusion by force of will but to develop a skill to look at all the evidence, both for and against our thoughts. When we take this approach to our inner thought lives, we often find that the evidence for any one conclusion is mixed. I'm not all good or all bad, and neither are others. Sometimes people are happy with me; sometimes they aren't. Sometimes I get the answer right, and sometimes I get it wrong. Sometimes I succeed, and sometimes I fail. Sometimes the scary thing I thought would happen happens, but more often it doesn't. And if the evidence is mixed, it means the extreme thing I tell myself can't be true. Helping our children understand this information is often enough to help them forgive themselves and others and keep moving forward with hope and bravery.

Step 3: Actions. Helping our children map out their feelings and the thoughts that go with those feelings is a tremendous gift. When we do this, we equip them to read the map of their own minds, and the minds of others, for themselves. We teach them how to make sense of powerful experiences that are confusing and at times scary. And most of all, we communicate to them that they are not alone or abnormal and that everyone, including grown-ups, has intense feelings and irrational thoughts. But there is one more thing you have to offer that will equip your child: an action plan.

Sometimes the "what's next" is obvious once you've sorted out the messy feelings and thoughts that led to an emotional storm, but sometimes it's not. When it's time to step forward again, many of the rules for boundaries also apply to equipping. Think in terms of natural consequences as much as possible, when consequences seem merited. With emotional storms, the issue is often not about consequences but about working with your child to imagine a path that helps them regain hope—a foothold for their situation that will allow them to move ahead. Help them brainstorm options by saying things like, "Why don't you try . . ." or "How about we just . . ." Sometimes you'll need to say something a little more forceful, like "I want you to at least try . . ." or "You're going to need to ____ before you can do these other things".

Step 4: Repair. Sometimes our kids' storms involve them hurting others. In those cases it is impossible to move forward in a healthy way without first seeking to make things right. I like to call this step Repair, but most people recognize it as "The Apology." Many parents make their children apologize and make up, saying something like, "Go apologize to your sister!" We insist on apologies out of the sense or belief that repair in relationships is important, which it is. Unresolved conflict and interpersonal pain are major life stressors, and having peace restored in a relationship is emotionally relieving and healing. But a coached "sorry" rarely does the job of promoting meaningful relational repair. Little kids, who are naturally forgiving and concrete in their thinking, will make good use of it. But once children are past the age of four or five, they are sophisticated enough to know that something more is required to repair a relationship.[5]

Instead of telling your child to apologize, learn to say, "You're going to need to make things right." At first they may need your help to translate "make things right." You can ask what they would need if they had been the one hurt and then encourage them to act in that direction. If the damage done to a relationship is severe, you may need to give them more direct instruction, like, "As part of making things right, you need to take money out of your allowance to pay for the toy you broke." But don't limit your child's repair to a checklist you provide. I think you'll be amazed at your child's innate ability to translate "make things right." And because your child's repair will be a genuine expression rather than a script you've given him, the other person involved is much more likely to receive it as an act of peace.

Ways We Abandon Our Children on the Trail

Many parents want to believe that if their children would just learn to obey the right rules for living, all their pain and messy emotional stuff would be avoided. And so some parents legislate their kids' behavior and incentivize following their rules. In our journey metaphor, this is the equivalent of saying, *Just stick to the trail, and you won't get hurt.* The "just do it" mentality is deep in our cultural mind-set, both inside and outside of faith communities. In this way of thinking, individuals are always to blame for their own problems. People are responsible for getting themselves "back on track" and shame is a constant companion of pain. If we embrace this mind-set, we miss the opportunity to help our children understand themselves and see new options when they get themselves into trouble. We also risk getting stuck in anger and resentment about their choices and feeling like failures ourselves.

Another mind-set that leaves our children alone on the trail is the impulse to treat them as equals, leaving them on their own to sort out the "what's next." Parents who embrace this way of thinking often believe they are respecting their child's autonomy by letting them find their own way, but leaving your child to wander aimlessly is as problematic as rigidly dictating what he needs to do and how he needs to do it.

I know that comfort and equipping can seem like overwhelming or exhausting tasks. This is why some parents are inclined to leave their child alone or skip straight to consequences and directives when their child is struggling. Please understand that providing comfort and equipping does not necessitate an hour-long therapy session over every emotional struggle and setback. In fact, doing so would be counterproductive. For older children in particular, time and space with an open door to talk as needed ("I am here to talk if and when you need me") is itself an act of genuine comfort. It is good for your child to work through some things herself, and failing to process every upsetting and distressing event in her life will not damage her. When you do attend to the need for comfort and equipping, realize that both can often occur in the space of a two-minute hug and three well-timed sentences. "I suspect you're disappointed . . ." *Hug.* "I know you were hoping things would turn out differently." *Pause.* "How about we make some time to practice this weekend before you try again?" But there will be times when taking the time to dig deeper will be worth the effort.

Curiosity and reflection, not having all the right answers, are the hallmarks of equipping. When you find yourself lost in the woods, the best thing to do is to stop, take a breath, look around, and gather your bearings. Review the terrain you've travelled. Reassess where you are headed and the experiences you've had in similar circumstances. Chart a wiser path forward. Be open to the task of equipping, and don't let it overwhelm you, remembering that it is your presence on the journey that matters to your child more than anything.

The Value of Discernment

Jesus's most famous collection of teachings is known as the Sermon on the Mount. In it, he teaches about how to live in a way that benefits both you and your neighbor. He ends his sermon by declaring, "Therefore everyone who hears these words of mine and puts them into practice is like a wise man who built his house on the rock. The rain came down, the streams rose, and the winds blew and beat against that house; yet it did not fall, because it had its foundation on the rock."[6]

During this sermon, Jesus addresses his listeners' emotional realities. Their proneness to anger and their lust, resentment, and pride. Jesus points out their jealousy and need for attention, and he *explicitly* names the worries and fears that underlie all those things. His listeners' emotions, and the thoughts that go with them, are essential context to Jesus. He invites his listeners to consider what they are feeling and thinking and how those thoughts and feelings might be destructive to them and others.

But naming the inner life is not enough. Jesus then offers hope by giving his listeners practical *actions* to take as they navigate through their emotional problems. Jesus invites them to a new way forward.

We are no different from Jesus's first listeners, and his words equip us to discern the difference between someone who would lead us toward life and someone who would lead us away from it. He tells us that there will be people who come to us in sheep's clothing, who seem to have our best interests at heart but who are in fact "ferocious wolves" set on using us for their own gain.[7] His wisdom was simple. "By their fruit you will recognize them."[8]

At this moment in history, when facts are muddied and we are being bombarded with a constant stream of often confusing, conflicting information, our children need us to help them develop discernment more than ever. They need us to teach them how to navigate a complicated world that is full of difficult emotions and conflicting ideas about what is right and good. Jesus's sermon shows no discernible concern for determining who is "in" or who is "out." It is a sermon about the immense challenge of living here and now in a hard and confusing world. We are wise to follow his lead in pressing in to that challenge with our children with both humility and urgency.

Reality Check

To get a general idea of how responsive you are to the need for equipping, look at the following diagram, and consider how prone you are to lean toward one side or the other. Consider asking your parenting partner, a friend, and/or your child to rate you as well. Differences in ratings are opportunities for insight and learning.

Equipping

NEED TYPE: GUIDANCE

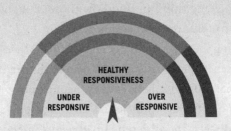

Here are some statements that may feel true if you tend to underrespond to the need for equipping:

- I don't have much to say about my child's worries or the conflicts she gets into. She'll need to figure out how to do the right thing on her own.
- If my child gets into trouble, I usually take over and fix the problem for him.
- I find myself lecturing my child about what she should do in the future if she's gotten herself into trouble or into conflict with someone.

Here are some statements that may feel true if you tend to overrespond to the need for equipping:

- When something has gone wrong for my child, I insist that we talk it out until I know exactly what happened and why and I'm confident she has learned from the experience and knows what to do next time to prevent it from ever happening again.
- I feel it is important to develop a specific action plan with my child about how he intends to follow up and make things right if he has trouble with someone.
- I am uncomfortable with letting my child decide what actions to take after an upset when it's clear what action I think she should take.

Small Steps to Take Today

If you lean toward being underresponsive to your child's need for equipping, consider how much further along in this journey of life you are than your child. You have probably been through a lot—heartache and disappointment and learning how to make peace with yourself and others. None of us have all the answers, but you've spent a lot of years navigating a complicated world and dealing with thoughts and feelings that are hard to untangle. If your temptation is to tell your kid what to do in the form of a directive like "You just need to . . ." consider taking a different tact. Invite your child into your process by describing experiences you've worked or struggled through yourself. Children love hearing stories about our own lives, and your kid is much more likely to listen to your wisdom if you share it through story rather than simply telling him what he should or should not do.

If you lean more toward overresponding to equipping, you might find yourself prone to overdoing life lessons and wanting to talk through every emotional outburst, conflict, and relational fracture. Step back a bit, and consider whether your eagerness to find solutions is a way of avoiding emotional pain. Sometimes we have to remind ourselves to slow down. Shortcuts often leave us lost and frustrated. Follow the compass. Comfort first, then equipping.

When you sense your child is struggling with something, extend the invitation to talk, but be willing to step away if the invitation isn't accepted. Respect that there may be some things that she needs to work out on her own or with others. This is especially true as our children grow into adolescence. Trust that if you have made it safe for your child to talk with you about hard things, she will likely eventually want your help or input, but on her own terms. Your kid might knock on your door late at night or start sharing something important just as you are dropping him off at school. Make room for those inconvenient and unexpected moments.

If your kid isn't sharing, it doesn't mean they don't want to be close to you—they might just not know how to reach you or don't believe you'll think what they have to say is important. Making time for walks, regular breakfast dates, or shared hobbies when you're not in crisis mode will create opportunities for you to speak wisdom into your kid's life when they need it most.

A SUSTAINABLE PATH OF CONNECTION

AMY

The Work of Remembering: A Story of Listening for Wisdom

During our time in New Zealand, we've learned to sing new songs. Some are in English and some are in te reo Māori, the first language spoken in this land. As I sing, I twist my tongue in new ways and stumble to teach my mind to read *wh* as my mouth forms the sound for *f*. Our boys, who pick up words and accents quickly, laugh at my attempts at pronunciation, but I'll keep trying, trusting that one day these new-to-me words will become familiar.

While the Māori language was the predominant language in Aotearoa, or New Zealand, in the early 1800s, by the mid-1900s, it was only spoken in Māori communities. And the Māori people, people who had settled in Aotearoa long before European settlers arrived, had seen their populations decimated. Children who attempted to speak te reo Māori in school were even beaten and forced to speak English.[1] In 1987, in an attempt to recognize this painful history and to begin to restore some of what had been lost, New Zealand made te reo Māori an official language.[2] Now a national movement is growing to teach the Māori language and to honor its importance. Schools incorporate te reo into their lessons, and I notice my boys beginning to sprinkle their language with Māori greetings. "Kia Ora, whānau!" has become a familiar hello in our home.

The boys sometimes must begin their school presentations with a Māori introduction of themselves, or *mihimihi*. The Māori culture places high value on connection to the land and to our ancestors, so the boys must begin by naming a mountain and river close to where they are from and include Jeffrey and me and their grandparents in their introductions. As they prepare to stand before their classmates, they ask me questions the mihi brings up for them. "I was born close to the James River, right, Mom? Is that where I should say we are from? Did you grow up where your parents live now? And where did our family belong before that?" The questions embody a yearning to know—*Who are you, Mom? And who does that make me?*

A product of my American culture, I feel myself forever pressing on to see what I can make of myself, rarely stopping to wonder where I've been and how it has shaped me. But my history informs who I am and who my children are becoming. Whether we acknowledge it or not, we are all deeply connected to the places we've been and to the people who've gone before us. Bringing that knowledge into the light by recognizing our histories and the role they play in our lives right now can be a powerful, essential instrument of healing. It allows us to both celebrate the beauty, love, and work of our parents and their parents before them and to count the cost of things that were hard. Acknowledging all of this together can lead us toward an authentic path of connection, repair, and restoration.

I can live in Aotearoa, this beautiful country of New Zealand, but if I ever want to fully inhabit it, I must open myself up to a language unfamiliar to me. That is how I can understand the country's history and participate in its path of healing. I'm learning to listen to Māori wisdom and to honor the work of remembering.

The words to one of our new songs are written in both English and te reo—

> Tuhia ki te rangi (Write it in the sky)
> Tuhia ki te whenua (Write it in the land)
> Tuhia ki te ngākau o ngā Tāngata katoa (Write it in the hearts
>   of all people)
> There is but one love
> And it is your love
> Ko te mea nui (The most important thing)
> Ko te aroha (Is love)[3]

As I open my mouth to sing, I wonder if entering into this newness is a form of speaking in tongues. Releasing myself into the language of another, feeling the sense of the words and exploring their contours beyond the confines of anything I know allows me to inhabit another's experience of God. I see God with new eyes—wider, truer, more connected. I would like to believe that this allows me to connect with a deeper language as well, a language alive within us all. It is the language of wisdom, a language that calls me to remember the song of where I'm from and to surrender to all that it has to teach me.

There will be moments in all of our lives when we have to know who we are. Times when we encounter real evil or are overwhelmed with deep, heartrending pain. Moments when it seems impossible to go on or the path of Love just feels too hard.

We tell our boys that there will be times when they feel fear and darkness pressing in—moments when they think they're all alone. These moments happen to all of us, and they are the times we must search deep inside and find our North Star. If you listen hard enough, you'll feel it wanting to lead you. Trust its direction. Let yourself align to where it wants to take you.

This is what the compass of connection is for. It can direct you to your own real place of need too and align you with wisdom that whispers, *You are safe. Do not fear. Keep going.* Or, *Come be still and rest for a while. Consider where you've been and all you've learned before you move ahead.* Even when you feel most alone, the Spirit is there, guiding you to your life's intersection of purpose, good relationships, and true exploration. Learn to recognize its voice, and let it lead you on.

JEFFREY

As we've studied the needs together, we've given you six directions to move in and explained how the compass can show you where you can turn in your relationship with your child. Just as a compass points all over the map, as a parent, you may often feel pulled in multiple, seemingly opposite, directions. It is less important to figure out an exact right way to go or which exact need to meet in the moment than it is to understand your options. We want you to be confident enough to switch directions when you feel disconnected or stuck. When your child feels safe and the world seems wide open with possibility, you can turn to delight, support, and boundaries. And when the world becomes stressful and overwhelming to your child, you can to turn to protection, comfort, and equipping to recover and reorient yourselves. Recognizing and meeting these needs, however imperfectly, will build intimacy and connection to last a lifetime.

We hope you'll find the six needs we've described to be a helpful and trustworthy way to navigate through the scientific and spiritual truths we've studied. Neither science nor faith offer failproof scripts about how to be a parent. Yet they do have much to say in common about what healthy relationships and human thriving look like. To us, this shared wisdom is a source of both hope and encouragement.

You have natural tendencies that will cause you to turn to certain needs over others, and your child will gravitate toward specific individual needs as well. As we discussed in chapter three, our natural temperaments and earliest experiences imprint these tendencies within us. We learned which needs were most likely to be met, and how, in our own early attachment relationships. We also learned which needs were most likely to be ignored and disregarded. We carry those lessons deep within us, whether we are conscious of them or not.

At the end of each of the chapters, and again in appendix A, we've provided diagrams for each of the needs to help you become more actively aware of your own tendencies. Under each diagram, you'll find examples of both under and overresponding behaviors and attitudes for each of the needs except delight, where we encourage you to be highly responsive. Most of us will see ourselves responding in these "too much" or "too little" ways at least some of the time. Knowing which needs we might over or under emphasize allows us to become wiser when things aren't going well, as does remembering that the sweet spot for each of the needs is in the middle. Aim high for delight, but for the rest, average is good. As you rate yourself, please don't forget that the goal isn't to be a perfect parent who always knows what their child needs and meets those needs perfectly. Instead the goal is to recognize your options and your own tendencies, and to develop the flexibility and openness to move in different directions when what you're offering doesn't seem to be helping your child.

The Gift of Good Enough

British pediatrician D. W. Winnicott famously introduced the concept of the "good enough mother," describing how healthy children develop resiliency from *not* having every distress or frustration immediately attended to and relieved.[4] Meeting and satisfying your child's every perceived need is not the path to health, happiness, and resilience. Let every parent rejoice! But even aiming for "good enough" can feel like an epic struggle some days (and even some years). When you feel that you are struggling to reach even a basic level of responsiveness to your child's needs, it can be helpful to recognize the three big factors that make being a parent so hard sometimes.

Your Wellness (or Lack Thereof)

Sick, tired, stressed out people are rarely the best versions of themselves. This is especially true for people who are parenting. Children are relentless. Their needs, dependence, and energy are relentless, and the trouble they get themselves into is often relentless too. It is essential that you recognize that self-care is a necessary part of caring for others. Most of us are familiar with the safety instructions on an airplane. In the case of a sudden loss of cabin pressure, put on your own oxygen mask first before trying to help the people around you. Parenting can sometimes feel like living at thirty thousand feet in a cabin without air pressure, especially if you have young children or a child with a disability or developmental challenges. Put your own mask on first since you may not be able to help your child otherwise. Caring for yourself also teaches your children that they are not at the center of the universe. They will survive and even benefit from seeing you attend to your own needs.

Sometimes we may find ourselves not well for more chronic reasons, such as clinical depression, anxiety, trauma, or substance dependence. Or we may be dealing with chronic relationship strain, whether an estranged marriage, a toxic work environment, or caring for an aging parent. No matter how hard you may be working to protect your children from these stressors, they will be affected by them. If this is your situation, I strongly encourage you to seek out support and get professional help if necessary. Your children need you to get the help you need and deserve.

Your History

*Just as your child has an attachment to you, you once were a child with attachments to your primary caregivers. **You** were on a journey with **them**.* Many of us have experienced returning home on the holidays as grown adults and slipping into patterns of thought, feeling, and action that seem straight from our childhoods. For some of us, this is comforting. For others, it is reason to keep our holiday visits short, if we travel home at all. Before you formed your first conscious memories, you already had at least three years of being in the world alongside your parents or the parent figures in your life. They responded to your needs for delight, support, and boundaries in whatever ways they knew best. They also responded to your needs for protection, comfort, and equipping as well as they could. Undoubtedly, they emphasized certain needs over others on the basis of their own histories, personalities, and the wisdom of their age. Whatever patterns they fell into, you fell into those patterns *with* them and carried them forward into your childhood.

The habits of behavior and emotional expression that you established with your primary attachment figures have become a largely unconscious script. There may have been times in your relationships with either or both of your parents when you tried to rewrite your relational script: to act and react within your relationship in new ways. Or conversely, there were periods when your parents radically rewrote the script for how you were going to navigate life together in regard to these six needs. But even if there were certain changes to the relational scripts we grew up with, you and I both are still carrying the habits of the intimate attachment relationships we learned along the way.[5]

These long-ago scripts for how the journey goes in an attachment relationship are imprinted onto all of us, and this programming exerts a powerful influence on our relationships with our kids, even when we consciously want the script to go differently. In other words, we don't get to parent from a blank slate. It just doesn't work that way. And that's okay, even if the script you inherited from your attachment figures is less than ideal. As long as you grow to be more conscious of the biases you inherited, you can transform the script into something healthier and more life-giving for you *and* your child.

To help you become more aware of what biases you have inherited from your attachment figures, I encourage you to return to the six needs diagrams and consider where you think each of your caregivers may have fallen in meeting those needs in you. You might even consider how their parents (your grandparents) met the six needs for them.

When I was growing up, my primary attachment figures emphasized support, boundaries, and protection in my life. I am grateful they met those needs well. The meeting of those needs helped me to be independent at a young age and to have a healthy respect for others that has served me well in life. Because this was the script I inherited growing up, I tend to jump to those same needs when parenting my own children, even when what my kids need is actually delight or comfort. Unfortunately, I have a hard time recognizing and valuing the need for delight and comfort—in myself as well as for my children—because those needs usually were not attended to in me when I was a child.

Because I have come to understand how important delight and comfort are, I am able to make the conscious effort to work on meeting those needs in my boys. But for me it has to be conscious. And often that conscious choice is made after I have pushed into the wrong need for the moment and things have fallen apart for my son and me. We get lost and stuck in turmoil over something, and as I feel the disconnect, I remember, *Oh, I'm going down the path I always go down, but my child doesn't need more boundaries right now. He needs my comfort first. My child needs me to go in a different direction to get back on track.*

Fear

All of us have fears as parents, and fear can dictate our relationships with our children and drive us to move in unhealthy directions. All the parents I meet have a deep yearning for things to turn out well for their children. But we all risk getting held captive, and holding our children captive, to fear. Especially when fears are unconscious, we can let them dictate our relationships with our kids and drive us to move in certain directions with them *right now!*

When I talk with parents about difficult situations they are facing with their child, I often ask, "What are you afraid of?" Some parents are able to articulate right off the bat what their fears are, and we can explore those fears from there. Other parents have trouble with the question.

When I use the word *fear*, I don't necessarily mean "scared," although that is exactly what some parents are feeling. I simply mean, "What outcome are you trying to keep from happening?" A child who doesn't obey right away? A boy who cries when he is sad or hurt? A girl who gets teased for being more interested in sports than dresses? A child who might get hurt climbing too high up a tree? A child who follows the path of a family member who has lived a difficult life?

Once parents are able to understand the question and begin to articulate their fears, I can ask follow-up questions: What will it mean if that thing you fear does happen? Will it mean you have failed as a parent? Or that others will think you have failed? That your child will end up unwilling to get a job and never leave the house? That your son will get beat up for being too sensitive? That your daughter will be permanently disabled if she gets hurt? That God will condemn your child for not believing the things you believe? Once we've explored those questions for a bit, it's time to explore these: Are those feared outcomes realistic or necessarily true? What makes them seem like they are?

Like many parents, Amy was worried when one of our boys seemed to fall behind in learning to read when he was little. I have my own set of fears, but this just wasn't a fear of mine. As she discussed her internal pressure to over-support our son's slowly emerging reading skills, we talked about the fact that neither one of us have a family history of learning disorders and that our son seemed interested and engaged in things other than reading. I was sure that one day he would be able to read, and whether he started at the same time as the rest of his peers didn't seem relevant to the future goal of literacy. If he was not meant to excel academically, his other interests assured me he would be able to find work and purpose in other areas of life. And wouldn't you know it, the next year our boy became a voracious reader. He just needed time. Had we pushed too hard too fast, he might have come to resent reading because of the negative associations of failure and pressure.

Some of us may be more driven by spiritual or moral fears. Our own experiences navigating a confusing, hurtful, or dangerous world have led many of us to rely on faith. These values and beliefs have become key to our own emotional survival and thriving. We may fear that if we give our children too much room to ask questions, challenge, and at times reject our faith and values, they will become lost in the world. In extreme cases, fear and social pressure reinforcing such fear can be crippling, which leads us to control our children's spiritual paths in ways that, ironically, are more likely to drive them away from the spiritual beliefs and experiences we want for them.[6] If you are a person of faith, try to rest in the hope that God is much bigger than we are, and the love that carries us is able and sufficient to see and carry our children too. Your child will need to find God on their own terms. We can support our children's exploration and give them tools for their journeys, but we cannot expect forced beliefs to be meaningful and life-giving for them. Try to enter into their questions without fear, and give them space to work out their beliefs on their own terms.

My observation is that many of our fears are tied to outcomes way off in the future, as if moving away from a direct line or road pointed to some future destination means that you will never get there. But if you have ever journeyed in nature, you know that you are rarely moving in a straight line toward your destination. Wisdom comes from knowing when to follow the contours of the land, even if it means moving away from your desired end point for a while, and when to make the hard climb over difficult terrain. Many parents climb every mountain in their way when they could be patient and take the windier trail. This is when choosing a growth trust mind-set can pay such dividends in your relationship with your child. We are all wired to grow *over time* toward flourishing, competence, and interconnectedness eventually, even when none of those things appear to be occurring right this minute.

You have a deep connection with your child. You also have a deep knowledge about the world gained from navigating it for years. But it can be hard to differentiate between intuition, instinct, and fear. This is why it is so important to recognize and name your fears, as well as your attachment history biases, so that you can hold them up against your intuition and instinct. This ability to distinguish between fears, your own attachment history biases, and genuine intuition is a skill worth building, but it takes reflection and conversation with those who can look at your situation in an unbiased light.

Growing with Your Child

We've used the metaphor of a shared journey throughout this book. Based on universal human needs for growth, the six compass points represent options for directions to move in with your child. We think the compass is a particularly helpful navigational tool for the daily situations you find yourself in with your kid.

There is another metaphor we can use to describe a child's growth—the metaphor of a seed growing in soil. This metaphor is helpful when you want to step back from any given situation and assess the big picture of your relationship. Plant a seed in the ground and it will grow, even if the soil is nutrient-poor. But if we care about the plant and want it to reach its full potential, it makes sense to pay attention to how the soil is doing over time. If the plant appears to be suffering, and we know it's most likely to thrive if its soil contains a balance of necessary nutrients, then we may want to back off from the nutrients that are too plentiful or add in nutrients that are lacking. The nutrients represent the six needs, and when our kids struggle, we can make educated guesses about which nutrient levels are too high or too low for them to flourish. We can focus on supporting neglected nutrients for a while. For instance, if you think delight is in short supply in your relationship, you could spend a week withholding judgments, putting aside future fears, and noticing and expressing love for who your child is right now. You might not see new growth overnight, but soon enough you will know whether your efforts are bearing fruit.

Your journey with your child and the growth in your relationship are your own. While we can't know exactly what you'll need when you run into trouble, in appendix B you'll find a series of steps to use as a starting point for applying the principles in this book when things are hard. The steps we've provided give you an idea of how to determine which nutrient, or need, to focus on with your child when they are struggling.

Jesus and Peter: Connection across Brokenness

Jesus was not a parent. But he pointed people to the perfect love of his *Abba*, or Father God, the One who placed these needs in all of us. He lived with and guided his close companions, or disciples, and commanded an authority in their lives that was based on his care and love for them. They lived as a family and faced danger and heartbreak together. Jesus also sent the disciples out on their own journeys to share with others what God was doing to restore his shalom of hope and peace to a world that was brutal and precarious for those not in positions of power. This was most people, especially women, the poor, children, and those rejected by the religious authorities for not following the God-rules, as they defined them. These religious authorities had gained power by aligning with the political rulers of the day, who themselves were not at all faithful or religious. Jesus called these leaders "a brood of vipers"[7] for the burdens they placed on people and the poison of their teaching and example. For them, what mattered most was enforcing the rules, and they did this by force and shame if necessary. But for Jesus, what mattered most was that relationships reflected the shalom he came to proclaim. Relationships with God and with one another were paramount to him.

Within the intimate relationships he had, Jesus met each of the needs we have described in this book: delight, support, boundaries, protection, comfort, and equipping. Perhaps the most vivid demonstration we see of Jesus's working his way through the compass is in his relationship with one of his close disciples, Peter. Jesus first met Peter on the shores of the Sea of Galilee, where Peter was fishing with his friends. There Jesus saw Peter exactly how he was and declared that he wanted to be with him. Jesus's delight was apparent in a gift particularly wonderful to Peter—tips about where to catch more fish. Jesus then began the process of discipleship, calling Peter and the others to himself by telling them that from now on they would gather people instead of fish. He walked with them while he drew people to God and showed them how he drew close to God himself, often by finding a quiet place to retreat to and be still. His support was then evident in the instructions and structure he offered as he sent the disciples out to do their own work.

Peter was a man who was impulsive, presumptuous, and prideful.[8] But Jesus saw beauty and strength where others likely saw foolishness and untrustworthiness, calling Peter the rock upon which he would build his church.[9] In the three years he spent with Jesus, Peter was invited to exercise faith and responsibility. He walked on water and sank into the water. Jesus rebuked him for wanting to use power against others and comforted him after he failed. He protected him from storms and equipped him for new challenges.

Then, after all they had been through together, when Jesus was about to be led to his death, it was as if Peter had learned nothing. Jesus announced to the disciples that it was time for him to leave and that this leaving could not be avoided. He told Peter that he would deny that he even knew Jesus. Peter wouldn't accept it. He insisted in his own trustworthiness. He was going to be that rock. But Jesus did not need Peter's relational protection. Instead, he invited Peter into an act of spiritual comfort, to stay up and pray for Jesus while he wrestled in prayer with God. Three times during this night of struggle, Jesus came to Peter, and three times he found Peter asleep. And like so many of us, having failed at meeting a relational need, Peter tried to make up for it by offering to meet some other need. When the authorities came to arrest Jesus, Peter pulled out a sword to fight for him. At this, Jesus had to set a boundary, telling Peter to put away his sword. Likely hurt, angry, and afraid, Peter fled as the authorities came and took Jesus away to his death.

Still hiding but not wanting to be far from Jesus, Peter snuck in to watch Jesus's trial. People recognized him in the courtyard and called him out as a follower of Jesus. Three times people claimed that he knew Jesus, and three times Peter swore that he didn't "know the man."[10] As the roosters crowed with the morning light, Peter remembered that Jesus had said, "Before the rooster crows, you will disown me three times."[11]

Peter fell into shame and despair. But this is not how the relationship ended because Jesus wouldn't let it end there.

Days after his death, Jesus appeared to his friends alive. Peter was in his boat fishing when he thought he saw Jesus on the shore. His friends thought he was seeing things, but that didn't stop Peter from jumping into the water and swimming to shore to try to draw close to Jesus. On shore, he saw that Jesus had made a meal for him and his friends. Even though they were stunned and unsure about what was happening, the disciples accepted the comfort Jesus offered, sitting by the fire he had made and eating the fish and bread he had prepared. I hope that Peter allowed himself to feel God's delight when he pulled a net overflowing with fish onto shore. Did Peter notice that even after everything that had happened, rather than withhold blessing, Jesus gifted him with abundance?

After their meal together, Jesus invited Peter away from the others to talk. Was Jesus going to rebuke him for his relationship failure, perhaps? Was he going to set him straight and make sure he had learned once and for all to trust him? No. Respecting Peter's privacy and autonomy, Jesus invited Peter away from the others to repair their relationship. And the repair came not with rebukes but with invitations.

"Do you love me?" Jesus asked Peter.[12] Three times Jesus asked, giving Peter the chance to reclaim his three denials. He followed each affirmation by a boundary for their relationship. Jesus said, if you love me, "take care of my sheep."[13] He told Peter what a restoring love would look like in *their* relationship. And in coming days, Jesus would equip Peter with a Spirit to remind him of all Jesus had taught him and the courage and strength to live out his invitation.

This isn't a relationship based on religious rules. It is a relationship based on loving connection. A relationship with delight and support and boundaries and protection and comfort and equipping. A relationship that never gave up and forgave "seventy times seventy" times. A relationship that just kept working out what love looks like after love failed in practice. Because love *will* fail in practice until all things are made new someday. In the meantime, love just keeps journeying on through all points of the compass. Just like you and your child, and our Creator and you.

THE SECRET TO SECURE CONNECTION

AMY

Love Bigger than Ourselves: A Story of Repair

One of my earliest memories is from an afternoon I spent with my grandfather. We were standing together in front of his blackberry bushes at an old mountain property we called The Farm. I watched his weathered hands pull a berry from a branch and press it into my palm. He encouraged me to taste, and I still remember tart sweetness exploding on my tongue.

Something about this moment must have imprinted on me, making me believe that taking children to harvest juicy, ripe fruit from sun-warmed bushes is something a good parent would do. But as of last year I'd only taken the boys to pick berries twice in their lives. One sunny Saturday last summer, I decided to try again.

Things started off reasonably well on the afternoon of our

adventure. We left later than planned and the kids were on their screens longer than I wanted them to be, but we were all in a jovial mood as we set off. I made several wrong turns on the way to the blueberry farm, and our half-hour drive turned into an hour, but it was okay. We were together! Going berry picking! Things were looking good for the Olricks.

We arrived at the farm and grabbed our buckets, then drove another half mile to the fields. Only five other cars were in view as I pulled over to park alongside long rows of bushes heavy with fruit. The sun was shining down, and a mountain rose up in the distance in front of us. The day was all I could have hoped for and more. Everything felt too good to be true.

Only a wide, sludge-filled drainage ditch stood between us and the berries. Two small wooden bridges spanned the gully, and I told the kids to go ahead but to cross at a bridge. I would meet them as soon as I gathered our buckets. But as I turned back to the car, I saw the boys running right to the edge of the ditch.

"Guys! Cross at the bridge! I'll be right there," I called over my shoulder, distracted.

"Mom, can we jump? Please, can we jump?" They were drawn like flies to the obstacle, and they wouldn't stop pestering. Distracted and still rooting around in the car, I gave in. "Fine, just be careful, okay?"

From behind me, I soon heard two sets of big-boy feet hit the earth with solid thuds. My body turned before my mind caught up, subconsciously already aware of what was unfolding.

Splash. Sure enough, one little-boy set of feet did not cross the ditch.

I ran over to find Nathan stuck up to his chest in mud—mud I assumed to be full of field runoff, including fertilizer and feces. My anger came quick. Scrambling down to the ground to pull Nathan out, I looked up at the older boys with an icy gaze. Their expressions of worry instantly turned to defensiveness.

Wrenching Nathan out of the mud, I turned to the other two. "Why did you do that? Why did you push me to let you jump? I couldn't see how wide the ditch was, but you could. You *knew* this would be too wide for him. You're his brothers! Why weren't you looking out for him?"

As I spoke, I carried Nathan back to our minivan, covering myself with the assumed-feces-filled mud in the process. I hope I asked him whether he was okay, but I honestly can't remember. I was too busy fuming and looking for a towel and spare set of clothes in the car. There was nothing to be found except a random large winter coat (*Why?*), which would be of no help to us. After pulling off Nathan's shirt and shorts more brusquely than necessary, I tried to wipe him off with one of the plastic bags that had lined a blueberry bucket. "But now I'm in my underwear! I don't want to be in my underwear!" Tears fell down his face as he wailed.

"You'll be okay. Get back in the car. There's nothing to do now but go home. You can't pick berries in your underwear, so we have to go." I shot the other boys another angry glance and told them to climb back in the car too. They moved to sit as far away from me as possible. I slammed the car door. I hadn't been this angry in a long time.

Thinking about it now, my level of fury seems a bit ridiculous. Children jump and sometimes fall into mud. I don't always remember to pack extra clothes. Things don't go as planned, and somehow we still make it through. But my old lie of failure was rearing its ugly head. I was not really consciously thinking anything as I gathered the boys and got them back to the car—I was only feeling. But if emotions had words, I imagine mine would have been saying something like this:

> *Nothing you do ever works out. This wouldn't have happened if Jeffrey were here, and if it* had *happened, he would have brought spare sets of clothes because he always remembers everything. Nathan always feels left*

behind by his brothers, and that will probably ruin his life. You work too
much, and your kids are on screens too much, and of course today ended
up in failure because that's what happens to you, and your children suffer
for it. And not only do you not feed your kids enough organic food, now
Nathan is covered in who-knows-what and is probably poisoned. And
look at those five happy families picking blueberries together right next to
you. They all managed to make it across the drainage ditch, didn't they?
This place is so beautiful, but it is not for you or your family. Beauty like
this is inaccessible to you. Because of you.

I give you that inner glimpse into my mind to show you how,
in moments of stress and intensity, my feelings and emotions can
overpower any attempt at thinking or logic. Part of this is simply
because of who I am—I have a tendency to catastrophize. And part
of it is due to my own attachment history. Mental health issues have
deep roots in my family tree, and I grew up feeding on the fruit
of that brokenness—internalizing a displeasure with myself that
can border on contempt. That old trauma still wields power. Stress
triggers it, and seeing my little boy covered in runoff scrambled all
my old wires. My expectations of the day had also primed me for
disappointment. In my mind, I had a perfect memory to live up to,
and I'd also created some imagined, nonexistent "good parent" to
compare myself to, a parent who is the perfect balance of in-charge
and carefree and who always keeps her children from harm.

All of this came together to add up to one thing: condemnation. And as happens with most self-hatred, I turned it on my kids
because it was too painful to bear alone.

I slammed my car door and prepared to drive us home without
berries. I kept telling myself not to talk, but I could feel my next
eruption coming. It seemed impossible to make it home without
launching into another lecture. Then, as I started the car and shifted
into reverse, I looked out the windshield and saw a familiar figure
climbing out of the car in front of us. A seventh car had arrived and,

oddly enough, it was a friend and colleague of Jeffrey's pulling up to pick blueberries with her girls. We had only lived in New Zealand for several months and didn't know many people. And right at that moment, a good distance from home and in the middle of this rural blueberry field, one of my only friends had shown up. The surprise of this was notable enough to shake me out of my agitated state.

Hands on the wheel, I took a deep breath. Should I get out to say hello and see whether she could help get me through the moment, or should I drive away and not subject her to our miserable mess? Her pulling up at just that moment felt less like a coincidence and more like a divine intervention, so I decided to get out. "Guys, our friend Adina just got here. I'll be right back." I climbed out of the van without looking back at the boys.

"Oh, hey! You're here! How are you?" she called out as I approached, and I'm sure she wasn't prepared for all that tumbled out. I told her how I had wanted to have a nice day and that Nathan fell into the ditch and was covered in mud and how now we were going to leave without berries. Sympathetic, she called her kids over and asked them to share some of their clothes. They emphatically refused, which was a timely reminder that kids are kids no matter whom they belong to. Then she asked whether I had anything else to put Nathan in, and I remembered the winter jacket that I had found while rummaging in the van. "Just put him in that," she encouraged me. "Kids don't care, and you don't want to go home without berries."

I climbed back into the car and really looked at Nathan for the first time since the fall. My eyes rested on his tear-stained face, and he looked back at me in misery, mud-spattered and mostly naked in his booster seat.

"Oh, buddy. I'm so sorry you're covered with mud." Now that I had been able to pause, logic and fierce love for my kids had room to rush back in. I felt like I was returning to myself after my flood of emotions.

I turned to the back of the car to face the other boys as well. Prone to hyperbole, I got right to the point. "Boys. I think Adina may have just saved our family." They looked back at me, wary but curious. "She convinced me we should try again. Nathan, would you be up for putting on a big coat and picking berries in that?" Nathan nodded. "Okay, let's do that, then."

We piled out of the car, still feeling emotional, and walked silently together over to the berry bushes—this time over a bridge. The older boys went their own way, and Nathan and I joined my friend and her girls. Later, after my heart and head had cleared some more, I asked her to watch Nathan so I could go make things right with the other boys, or "repair" as Jeffrey likes to call it. He says that human relationships are bound to get bruised and broken, but kids make it through just fine and can even grow from difficult things, as long as we don't pretend nothing happened and are committed to repairing the situation with them. This is hard but hope-filled for me.

I found Josh and Drew filling their buckets on the next long row of berries, and I could still see the hurt in their eyes as I approached. "Guys, I want to check in with you. I do need you to listen and watch out for your brother, but my reaction was out of line. I wanted this day to be perfect, and seeing Nathan in the mud really upset me. I lashed out at you, and I shouldn't have. Will you forgive me for that?" The boys nodded yes and apologized for not looking out for Nathan. We gathered together for a mud-splattered embrace, right there among the blueberries. "Can you believe that our friends showed up when they did, right at that moment? Does it feel like a God moment to you the way it does to me?" I couldn't help asking them, wondering whether they found her arrival as remarkable as I did.

Josh nodded. "It really does, Mom. If she hadn't come right then, the trip home would have been so bad—we were all so mad at each other."

And so we made it through. With Nathan's mud-splattered body covered in a coat reaching his ankles, my little family and I filled up our buckets. I found my way home without getting lost. And the next day we discovered that sun-ripened, hand-picked blueberries taste even sweeter when they are piled on top of waffles with whipped cream and covered in grace.

When I was eighteen, I went to college happy to be away from God, relieved to be free from the judgment and punishments I'd been told were required by God to grow me. I decided that if I was going to make it on my own, I needed to start believing in myself, and that meant leaving God behind. But my new freedom gave me a chance to remember that there had been certain key times in my childhood when I'd felt God's protective presence in ways I couldn't explain away. I reasoned that if God was real, God was surely big enough to hear my questions. I began speaking my pain out loud as prayer and feeling a growing sense of peace and calm. I still couldn't bring myself to believe in God, but I started to wonder if God might believe in me.

The presence I was feeling was not an angry deity lording over me, but rather Love made known in the person of Jesus—someone who paid attention to women and children and had a particular heart for the broken. Church was a hard place for me to enter into though, so one Sunday morning I hiked up to Observatory Hill, a wooded area behind my dorm. I was looking to find God in nature, where I felt most free. I didn't see anyone else out on the trail, so I began speaking aloud as I walked—a wounded young woman, wandering alone in the woods and muttering. I remember saying something like, "Okay. You've got me. I believe in you now. I know I can't get away from you, and I don't even want to anymore. But you need to know this. I will *never* get married, and I will *never* have a family because I don't know how to love—I would hurt anyone I try to care for. So that's it. It's just going to be me and you. Got it?"

Dappled sunlight shone through the canopy of leaves above me, following me as I walked. And then a presence broke into my thoughts, not audible but as clear as the words I am writing right now, declaring to me that I was not alone. Love whispered aloud, and the question I heard was, "But haven't I made you a new creation?"

I had left home thinking there were parts of me beyond repair. I believed there were places within me forever broken and dead. But the question whispered to my heart invited me to remember—to remember that as a man, Jesus had been dead too. And as a man, even Jesus could not resurrect himself. No, he surrendered himself to the divine, and when all seemed lost, God breathed and raised him up again.

In that moment in the woods, I decided to hand myself over to God as well, to surrender to the power that promises to make all things new and resurrect the dead and calm every storm. I said yes to a Spirit that tells me that every day—every moment, even—is an opportunity to be born again.

I had no idea then that a little over a year later I would meet a tall, handsome graduate student named Jeffrey. Or that Jeffrey and I would embark on a life together that would give us three beautiful boys and lead to one sunny day in a blueberry field, where I was reminded that some resurrections happen all at once, and some, like mine, happen again and again. In cars filled with anger, in the middle of sleepless nights, in the moments you're feeling desperate and alone, resurrection can be an ongoing process. We're constantly being invited to surrender ourselves to Love bigger than ourselves. Grace offers us a forever invitation to rise again.

I invite you to entertain the breathtakingly hopeful idea that Love may be with you and for you and your children, not in spite of but because of who you are. Just like the way your kids' hair sticks up in the back and their silly, lopsided grins make you love them all the more. You love them not because they are perfect but because they are uniquely and wonderfully yours. Love delights in you the same way. We are all messy, imperfect and at times quite disappointing. But I truly believe that we are also unimaginably loved. And when we cry out, Love hears and draws us in close.

That day at the blueberry field, a jump into a drainage ditch destroyed my vision of perfection. Left to my own devices, the experience would have been a disaster. I like to believe that God saw through all that and saw us—me and my reactiveness and my angry little mud-covered family. Love entered into the mess and invited us to find the beauty that was still there. Instead of letting us sit in our anger and shame, God gave us a chance to pause and breathe and look around to see what was true. *This beauty is for you. Your lives are a gift. These kids are yours and you are mine. Return to each other and love each other. And see that I am always here with you, right in the middle of it all.*

JEFFREY

Dr. Mary Ainsworth's Strange Situation, the simple procedure that made it possible to study and describe the enduring influence of human attachment, lasts just twenty-one minutes. But the procedure's short interactions uncover the complex relational world that exists between a parent and child. Fear expressed or not expressed tells a story, as do hugs offered or withheld. A tiny glance away or a warm smile of welcome can speak volumes about the relationship between two people who love each other deeply. The way they move away from each other and come back together again paints a picture of how countless similar interactions spaced out over the course of a life together have gone and where they are likely to continue to go.

As a certified Strange Situation coder, I am trained to look for a wide variety of complex behaviors across the various episodes of the procedure. I watch for body language, tone of voice, the language that is used, eye contact, and how emotion is expressed or constrained. There is a lot that goes on in that twenty-one minutes that differentiates one parent-child relationship from another, and all of it is useful and important. But two moments stand out above all the rest in determining whether the child I am coding is secure in his attachment to his parent—the moments of reunion.

It is in these moments—when the parent returns after leaving her child with a stranger and again when she is reunited with her child left alone in an empty room—that the two of them show us the essential quality of their attachment. We get a glimpse into whether theirs is a relationship that is open and able to repair itself from the small fractures that all relationships experience every day. Do they reconnect and find a way forward together, or do these fractures leave them disconnected?

The secret to a secure relationship is not that there are no fractures, mistakes, misunderstandings, hurt feelings, or wrong turns. The secret to a secure relationship is for parents and children to face those fractures and wrong turns head-on, together. As I say to my clients, mistakes and missteps are not the measure of your parenting or your child. Those are inevitable and unavoidable. It's your willingness and ability to repair and reconnect after difficulty that demonstrates the strength of your relationship. The gift of a secure attachment comes about through returning to each other over and over again, even and especially when things get hard.

As you travel on, allow yourself to be on a journey with your child. Give yourself the freedom to run into trouble and get a little lost along the way. Don't fear if it suddenly seems like maybe you've taken a dead-end trail. It's okay to accumulate some bumps and bruises and get delayed and off course sometimes. Some of your best stories and greatest adventures will come from obstacles you'll encounter and overcome as you get where you need to grow. Remember the compass, and let it and the still, small voice within you show you a direction to take. Giving yourself the freedom to step off a predetermined path will open you up to worlds that exist within your child *and* you. You may be surprised at where Love wants to take you.

ACKNOWLEDGMENTS

To all the beloved family and friends who have invested so much love, generosity, and wisdom into our lives: words cannot express our gratitude for how you have carried us.

To our agent, Kathryn Helmers, who breathed life into our dream and made it come alive: this book is as much yours as it is ours.

And to our editor, Stephanie Smith: thank you for believing in these words and for working so hard to make them sing.

Jeffrey is especially indebted to his professional mentors, Drs. Patricia Crittenden, Robert Marvin, Robert Pianta, and William Whelan. Thank you for opening up my mind to the power of attachment and pouring out your knowledge and passion for the exploration of human connection: this book could not have been possible without all I have learned from you.

Finally, we bow in wonder to the One whose wild and tender Spirit has led us—through mountains and valleys and halfway around the world—together and to this work.

THE 6 NEEDS ASSESSMENT TOOLS

As you consider our needs assessment tools, you'll probably find you are highly responsive to some needs and less responsive to others. To get a general idea of how sensitive you are to each one, look over the diagrams and consider whether you tend to lean toward one side or the other. Consider asking your parenting partner, a friend, and/or your child to assess you as well. Differences in ratings are opportunities for insight and learning.

Delight

Need Type: Mirroring

Here are some statements that may feel true if you tend to underrespond to the need for delight:

- I don't seem to really notice my child unless he is doing something wrong or bothersome.
- It's hard to think of times recently when I truly enjoyed my child.
- I generally feel agitated and annoyed at my child when I'm in her presence.

Here are some statements that may feel true if you are highly responsive to the need for delight:

- I enjoy spending time with my child, playing and discovering with them.
- I enjoy finding out how my child sees and experiences the world, even when it's different from my view or experience.
- I enjoy seeing what interests or motivates my child even when those interests are different from my own.

Support

Need Type: Guidance

Here are some statements that may feel true if you tend to underrespond to the need for support:

- I prefer to let my child figure things out on his own.
- I am often too busy with my own work and activities to give much time to helping my child with theirs.
- When I try to help my child with something, I often end up feeling frustrated and walking away.

Here are some statements that may feel true if you tend to overrespond to the need for support:

- I am quick to jump in and show my child how things are done.
- I often take over a task for my child if I feel like he's not doing it right.
- I get really uncomfortable with the idea of my child failing or not reaching his full potential.

Boundaries

Need Type: Taking Charge

Here are some statements that may feel true if you tend to underrespond to the need for boundaries:

- I generally let my child have his own way.
- I tell my child what he can or can't do, but he does what he wants anyway.
- I go through periods of laying down the law but seem to have trouble following through.

Here are some statements that may feel true if you tend to overrespond to the need for boundaries:

- I have strong expectations and rules for how my child should act, and I enforce them.
- It is very important to me that my child learns to obey.
- I am willing to resort to severe punishment if my child is disobedient.

Protection

Need Type: Taking Charge

Here are some statements that may feel true if you tend to underrespond to the need for protection:

- I don't feel the need to pay too close attention to where my child is or whom she is with. She knows how to take care of herself.

- If my child wants to do something, I have a hard time saying no, even if the activity or situation makes me uncomfortable.
- If another adult puts my child in his place, he probably had it coming.

Here are some statements that may feel true if you tend to overrespond to the need for protection:

- I never leave my child alone with another adult unless I know that adult really well or have clear assurance of their safety.
- I feel very uncomfortable letting my child engage in physical activities or exploration if I think there is any chance he could get hurt.
- I'm not comfortable with letting my child spend too much time away from me with friends, even if I know and like the friends' families.

Comfort

Need Type: Mirroring

Here are some statements that may feel true if you tend to underrespond to the need for comfort:

- My first instinct is to assure my child that he is all right unless he's clearly hurt badly.
- I find it uncomfortable to linger in a hug with my child, to hold hands, or to otherwise engage in extended acts of affection.
- I tend to distract myself when I am upset about something, and I do the same for my child if they are upset.

Here are some statements that may feel true if you tend to over-respond to the need for comfort:

- I feel the need to touch, hold, and soothe my child at the first signs of distress or discomfort, whether or not he asks for it.
- I have trouble letting my child move away from me if I am unsure whether the hurt she is carrying is truly gone.
- I always try to make my child talk to me about what is going on inside her if she looks upset or doesn't seem like her normal self.

Equipping

Need Type: Guidance

Here are some statements that may feel true if you tend to underrespond to the need for equipping:

- I don't have much to say about my child's worries or the conflicts she gets into. She'll need to figure out how to do the right thing on her own.
- If my child gets into trouble, I usually take over and fix the problem for him.
- I find myself lecturing my child about what she should do in the future if she's gotten herself in trouble or into conflict with someone.

Here are some statements that may feel true if you tend to over-respond to the need for equipping:

- When something has gone wrong for my child, I insist that we talk it out until I know exactly what happened and why and I'm confident she has learned from the experience and knows what to do next time to prevent it from ever happening again.

- I feel it is important to develop a specific action plan with my child about how he intends to follow up and make things right if he has trouble with someone.
- I am uncomfortable with letting my child decide what actions to take after an upset when it's clear what action I think she should take.

Once you've assessed how you tend to respond to the needs, engage in the below questions and exercises:

Question 1: Were there major differences in how you see yourself and how your partner or child sees you?

Exercise 1: If some major differences exist, do they seem to be due to confusion about what the dimensions mean, or do they seem to be due to genuine differences between how you view yourself and how others see you as a parent? Are you able to talk about these differences productively, or do you feel threatened and defensive about any differences of opinion?

Question 2: Which needs did you rate yourself as being prone to underrespond or overrespond to? Leaning toward overresponsiveness means you see and highly value that need in your child. Leaning toward underresponsiveness means you may have difficulty recognizing or seeing the true value of that need in your child.

Exercise 2a: Look at the needs you are prone to overrespond to and be grateful. Your attention to those needs is a gift to your child. But also reflect on how overemphasizing and overresponding to those needs may sometimes be "too much of a good thing." (Unless it's delight. Don't hold back there!) Consider how your attention to the needs you're good at attending to may hinder your child in areas where other needs may be present. Consider asking your child whether he feels like you overdo it with certain things. For support you might ask, "Do you think I help too much with things, things you think you can handle yourself?" With boundaries, "Do you think our rules are too strict or too hard to keep?" With protection, "Are there things you'd like to do that you don't think I would allow but that you feel like you could handle?" With comfort, "Do you think I overdo it with asking how you're feeling or trying to make you feel better?" With equipping, "Do you think I overdo helping you figure out how to handle conflicts and setbacks?"

If the idea of backing off a little in a need that you highly attend to feels uncomfortable, consider why that may be. Consider your personal history and also what fears you might have about what would happen to your child if you were to pull back from that need just a little. Where might those fears be coming from, whether from your personal history or from the world around you?

Exercise 2b: Look at the needs you are prone to underrespond to, and become curious about why you might have difficulty noticing or valuing those needs in your child. In particular, consider how those needs were met, or not met, for you as a child. Many people assume that how they respond to their child is an inborn personality trait (e.g., "I'm just not a touchy-feely person"), but you may find that it simply wasn't modeled for you in your relationships growing up, so meeting the need feels unfamiliar or uncomfortable for you.

Need Dimensions

Mirroring: Delight and Comfort

Guidance: Support and Equipping

Taking Charge: Boundaries and Protection

Food for Thought

Remember that more attention toward a need is not always better. To show you how both over- and underattending to certain needs can create problems, we've put together a list of some common parenting styles and how they engage certain needs specifically. You've probably heard of most of the types on the list and may even identify with one or two. If so, consider how you could bring your relationship into more balance by focusing on some of the needs you're not attentive to or by de-emphasizing some of the needs you overattend to. Can you think of other well-known parenting styles and how they might interact with the needs?

Playmate Parent: High Delight, Low Boundaries

Permissive Parent: Low Boundaries, Low Protection

Authoritarian Parent: Low Delight, High Boundaries, Low Comfort

Helicopter Parent: High Support, High Protection, High Equipping

Free-Range Parent: Low Support, Low Equipping

Achievement-Pusher Parent: Low Delight, High Boundaries, High Support, Low Comfort

STEPS TO TAKE IF YOUR CHILD IS STRUGGLING

1. Start with Protection

Ask yourself, "Is it possible my child feels unsafe physically or emotionally?" If she is feeling unsafe or has been hurt, immediately **comfort** her, then take whatever action is necessary to protect her from further harm.

Things to Consider:

- If the source of harm is coming from another family member, get help from a trusted family member, medical or mental health professional, or the police.
- If the knowledge that your child has been feeling unsafe or has been hurt feels paralyzing or overwhelming to you, get help yourself from a mental health professional.
- If your child is still struggling after you have moved to protect and comfort her, consider seeking out a mental health professional to rule out specific depressive or anxiety disorders.

2. If Your Child Is Feeling Safe, Focus Next on Delight

If your child is safe but struggling, make it a priority to create time and space to simply enjoy and play with him. Look him in the eye, and tell him how much you love and enjoy him. Be specific about the things you appreciate about him as a person. Take the time to write a letter to him or a postcard with the top ten things you love about him that he can pin up on his wall or carry with him in his backpack. Be careful not to slip into pride or approval about his accomplishments or abilities. "I love watching you climb the monkey bars" sends a different message than "I love that you are a good climber." The latter implies that your love depends on him being "a good climber."

If delight is hard for you, press into prayer and even therapy to explore why this might be the case. Look at your hopes, dreams, and expectations. Work through grief and fears you may have. Give yourself permission to accept that your child has a difficult personality for you and that this doesn't make you a bad parent.

Temperament, irritability, rigidity, and extreme moodiness are major challenges to delighting in a person. Enlist the help of a psychologist if you suspect that your child's challenges may be due to developmental concerns such as Autistic Spectrum Disorder, Obsessive Compulsive Disorder, ADHD or ADD, or sensory processing disorders, especially if there is any family history of similar concerns.

3. If Protection and Delight Are Settled, Focus Next on Boundaries

Explore the basis for your demands and expectations for your child. Are there too many? Are they unclear or inconsistent, or are they nonexistent?

Children struggle when they have too many or too few boundaries, and boundaries should be developmentally appropriate. You may think your child is capable of handling something and he's not, *or* you may think he's not yet capable of something and he is. Either will create problems.

Boundaries are often linked to expectations. Ask yourself: How much help does my child need to *regularly* meet my expectations? You may think that because your child has handled something once, he should be good to go. That's not always the case. It can help to ask other parents of children the same age to get a sense of what is reasonably possible and appropriate.

If you still have trouble figuring out developmentally appropriate boundaries for your child, work with your child using a collaborative problem-solving approach. This involves identifying together what your child feels he needs in the situation, naming what you need in the situation, and jointly finding a solution that addresses *both* sets of needs. Taking such an approach can feel very uncomfortable for parents who value their role as authority figures. If this is the case for you, know that taking such an approach is a profound form of leadership. Your child needs your help finding his own voice, understanding that his actions or inactions have consequences, and developing realistic solutions to conflicts. If you don't help him develop these skills, how will he learn them? We highly recommend the book *Raising Human Beings* by Ross Greene for a more detailed exploration of what this process looks like.

Enlist the help of a family therapist if needed.

If you are having trouble adjusting your expectations to your child's current capacities and maturity, it may be useful to get professional feedback. Feeling like you can't afford to adjust your expectations may be a sign of perfectionism, Obsessive Compulsive Disorder, Autism Spectrum Disorder, or some other anxiety disorder.

4. Lastly, Consider Whether Your Child Needs More Active Support and Equipping

Your last general-purpose strategy is to consider whether the reason your child is floundering is because she needs more guidance and practical hands-on help with tasks and life challenges.

Ask yourself: Are her school or peer interactions overwhelming? What are your child's mental habits and beliefs about herself? How does she talk to herself? What are her structures of organization and help-seeking? Does she seem to give up on things too easily or burn herself out without much to show for it? Does she seem overwhelmed?

She may need your support and equipping. Take time out in a nonthreatening context to talk about your observations that she seems like she's struggling, or that everything seems like a battle. Use a collaborative problem-solving approach to better understand how your child sees things and to clarify her and your priorities. First solicit your child's ideas for what would help her, rather than imposing solutions unilaterally. Ask her how she thinks you can help her. Offer ideas of how you think you might be able to help her. Agree to try out new strategies, and review in a week and adjust accordingly. Be open to outside sources of help if your child struggles to "let you" help her.

Enlist the help of a family therapist if needed.

STEPS TO TAKE IF YOU ARE STRUGGLING

Recognizing that you need help is hard. Seeking out that help is even harder. If you are struggling, please believe that simply reading these words and considering your options is a brave first step.

If you would like to find a counselor or psychologist to speak to, you can use this tool to discover licensed therapists in your area:

https://www.psychologytoday.com/us/therapists/

If you would feel more comfortable talking with a counselor over the phone or by video, **talkspace.com** and **breakthrough.com** are two websites that connect you with licensed therapists online.

Please be patient with yourself as you reach out for help, and know that it might take a few tries to find the right person or people to talk to.

If you need someone to talk to today, here is a list of reputable 24-hour hotlines:

- **National Suicide Prevention Lifeline:** 1–800–273–8255
- **The Rape, Abuse & Incest National Network (RAINN):** 1–800–656–HOPE (1–800–656–4673)
- **Childhelp,** a nonprofit dedicated to the prevention of child abuse: 1–800–4–A–CHILD (1–800–422–4453)
- **National Domestic Violence Hotline:** 1–800–799–SAFE (1–800–799–7233)

If you would like to find and join a group of people who are dealing with similar issues, here are a few places to start:

- Alcoholics Anonymous: http://www.aa.org
- Al-Anon provides help and hope for families and friends of alcoholics: https://al-anon.org
- Families Anonymous provides support and recovery from the effects of a loved one's addictions: http://www.familiesanonymous.org
- Depression and Bipolar Support Alliance: https://dbsalliance.org

For an online, up-to-date list of these resources, as well as recommended books and voices, visit our website at https://growingconnected.com.

NOTES

Chapter 1: Beyond Formulas and Fears

1. Alison Gopnik, *The Gardener and the Carpenter* (New York: Farrar, Straus & Giroux, 2016), 21.
2. Matthias Doepke et al., "The Economic Roots of Helicopter Parenting," Phi Delta Kappan 100, no. 7 (2019): 22–7.
3. Alfie Kohn, *Punished by Rewards: The Trouble with Gold Stars, Incentive Plans, A's, Praise, and Other Bribes* (Boston: Houghton Mifflin, 1993).
4. Daniel Siegel and Tina Payne Bryson, "'Time-Outs' Are Hurting Your Child," *Time*, September 23, 2014, http://time.com/3404701 /discipline-time-out-is-not-good/.

Chapter 2: The Science of Connection

1. John Bowlby, "Maternal Care and Mental Health," *Bulletin of the World Health Organization* no. 3 (1951): 355–534.
2. John Bowlby, *Attachment and Loss, Volume 1: Attachment* (New York: Basic, 1969).
3. Mary Ainsworth, Mary Blehar, Everett Waters, and Sally Wall, *Patterns of Attachment: A Psychological Study of the Strange Situation* (Hillsdale, NJ: Erlbaum, 1978).
4. Mary Ainsworth et al., "Attachment and Exploratory Behavior of One-Year-Olds in a Strange Situation," in *Determinants of Infant Behavior IV*, ed. Brian Foss (London, UK: Methuen, 1969), 113–36; Mary Main and Jude Solomon, "Discovery of a New, Insecure-Disorganized/Disoriented Attachment Pattern," in *Affective Development in Infancy*, eds. T. Berry Brazelton and Michael Yogman (Westport, CT: Ablex, 1986), 95–124.
5. Erin O'Connor, et al., "Risks and Outcomes Associated with Disorganized/Controlling Patterns of Attachment at Age Three in the NICHD Study of Early Child Care and Youth Development," *Infant Mental Health Journal* 32, no. 4 (July-August 2011): 450–72, https://doi.org/10.1002/imhj.20305; Mary Main, et al., "Categories of Response to Reunion with the Parent at Age 6: Predictable from Infant Attachment Classifications and Stable over a 1-Month Period," *Developmental Psychology* 24, no. 3 (1988): 415–526, https://doi .org/10.1037/0012-1649.24.3.415.
6. Marinus Van IJzendoorn, et al., "Cross-Cultural Patterns of

Attachment: A Meta-Analysis of the Strange Situation," *Child Development* 59, no. 1 (1988): 147–56; Marinus van IJzendoorn, et al., "Disorganized Attachment in Early Childhood: Meta-Analysis of Precursors, Concomitants, and Sequelae," *Development and Psychopathology* 11, no. 2 (June 1999): 225–50, https://doi.org/10.1017/S0954579499002035.

7. Jude Cassidy, "Emotion Regulation: Influences of Attachment Relationships," *Society for Research in Child Development* 59, nos. 2–3 (1994): 228–49, https://doi.org/10.1111/j.1540-5834.1994.tb01287.x.

8. Allan Schore, "Attachment and the Regulation of the Right Brain," *Attachment and Human Development* 2, no. 1 (2000): 23–47, https://doi.org/10.1080/146167300361309; Grazyna Kochanska et al., "The Development of Self-Regulation in the First Four Years of Life," *Child Development* 72, no. 4 (July/August 2001): 1091–111, https://doi.org/10.1111/1467-8624.00336.

9. Sara Waters et al., "Emotion Regulation and Attachment: Unpacking Two Constructs and Their Association," *Journal of Psychopathology and Behavioral Assessment* 32, no. 1 (March 2010): 37–47, https://doi.org/10.1007/s10862-009-9163-z; Ashley Groh et al., "The Significance of Attachment Security for Children's Social Competence with Peers: A Meta-Analytic Study," *Attachment and Human Development* 16, no. 2 (February 2014): 103–36, https://doi.org/10.1080/14616734.2014.883636; Michelle DeKlyen and Mark Greenberg, "Attachment and Psychopathology in Childhood," in *Handbook of Attachment, Third Edition: Theory, Research, and Clinical Applications*, eds. Jude Cassidy and Phillip Shaver (New York: Guilford, 2016): 639–66; Yael Dvir et al., "Childhood Maltreatment, Emotional Dysregulation, and Psychiatric Comorbidities," *Harvard Review of Psychiatry* 22, no. 3 (May/June 2014): 149–61, https://doi.org/10.1097/HRP.0000000000000014.

10. Valery Chirkov, Richard Ryan, and Kennon Sheldon, eds., *Human Autonomy in Cross-Cultural Context: Perspectives on the Psychology of Agency, Freedom, and Well-Being* (Amsterdam: Springer Netherlands, 2011).

11. Natasha Whipple et al., "Attending to the Exploration Side of Infant Attachment: Contributions from Self-Determination Theory," *Canadian Psychology* 50, no. 4 (November 2009): 219–29, https://doi.org/10.1037/a0016322.

12. Richard Ryan, Edward Deci, and Maarten Vansteenkiste, "Autonomy and Autonomy Disturbances in Self-Development and Psychopathology: Research on Motivation, Attachment, and Clinical Process," in *Developmental Psychopathology: Volume 1, Theory and Method*,

ed. Dante Cicchetti (Hoboken, NJ: Wiley & Sons, 2016), 385–438; L. A. Sroufe et al., *The Development of the Person: The Minnesota Study of Risk and Adaptation from Birth to Adulthood* (New York: Guilford, 2005); Maarten Vansteenkiste et al., "On Psychological Growth and Vulnerability: Basic Psychological Need Satisfaction and Need Frustration as a Unifying Principle," *Journal of Psychotherapy Integration* 23, no. 3 (2013): https://doi.org/10.1037/a0032359; Karin Grossmann et al., "A Wider View of Attachment and Exploration: The Influence of Mothers and Fathers on the Development of Psychological Security from Infancy to Young Adulthood," in *Handbook of Attachment, Second Edition: Theory, Research, and Clinical Applications*, eds. Jude Cassidy and Phillip Shaver (New York: Guilford, 2008), 857–79.

13. Katherine Ehrlich, "Attachment and Psychoneuroimmunology," *Current Opinion in Psychology* 25 (February 2019): 96–100, https://doi.org/10.1016/j.copsyc.2018.03.012.

14. Karlen Lyons-Ruth and Deborah Jacobvitz, "Neurobiological Correlates, Parenting Contexts, and Pathways to Disorder," in *Handbook of Attachment, Third Edition: Theory, Research, and Clinical Applications*, eds. Jude Cassidy and Phillip Shaver (New York: Guilford, 2016): 667–95; Martin Teicher, "Wounds That Time Won't Heal: The Neurobiology of Child Abuse," *Cerebrum* 2, no. 4 (January 2000): 50–67.

15. Miranda van Bodegom et al., "Modulation of the Hypothalamic-Pituitary-Adrenal Axis by Early Life Stress Exposure," *Frontiers in Cellular Neuroscience* 1,1 no. 87 (April 2017): 1–33, https://doi.org/10.3389/fncel.2017.00087.

16. Pim Cuijpers et al., "The Disease Burden of Childhood Adversities in Adults: A Population-Based Study," *Child Abuse & Neglect* 35 (November 2011): 937–45, https://doi.org/10.1016/j.chiabu.2011.06.005; Martin H. Teicher et al., "Sticks, Stones, and Hurtful Words: Relative Effects of Various Forms of Childhood Maltreatment," *American Journal of Psychiatry* 163 (June 2006): 993–1000, https://doi.org/10.1176/appi.ajp.163.6.993; Vincent Felitti et al., "Relationship of Childhood Abuse and Household Dysfunction to Many of the Leading Causes of Death in Adults," *American Journal of Preventive Medicine* 14, no. 4, (1998): 245–58, https//doi.org/10.1016/s0749-3797(98)00017-8. Mario Mikulincer et al., "An Attachment Perspective on Psychopathology," *World Psychiatry* 11, no. 1 (February 2012): 11–15, https//doi.org:/10.1016/j.wpsyc.2012.01.003.

17. Jeffrey Olrick, "Caregiving of Adoptive Parents in a Home-Based Separation and Reunion Procedure" (PhD diss., University of Virginia, 2001); Thomas O'Connor et al., "Child–Parent Attachment

following Early Institutional Deprivation," *Development and Psychopathology* 15, no. 1 (June 2003): 19–38, https://doi.org/10.1017/S0954579403000026.

18. Kent Hoffman et al., "Changing Toddlers' and Preschoolers' Attachment Classifications: The Circle of Security Intervention," *Journal of Consulting and Clinical Psychology* 74, no. 6 (December 2006): 1017–1026, https://doi.org/10.1037/0022-006X.74.6.1017.

19. Josh McDowell and Sean McDowell, *The Bible Handbook of Difficult Verses: A Complete Guide to Answering the Tough Questions (The McDowell Apologetics Library)*, (Eugene, OR: Harvest House , 2013), 140; Dannah Gresh, *The 20 Hardest Questions Every Mom Faces: Praying Your Way to Realistic, Biblical Answers* (Eugene, OR: Harvest House, 2016), 59; Albert Barnes, Notes on the Bible by Albert Barnes, 1834, https://biblehub.com/commentaries/barnes/proverbs/22.htm.

Chapter 3: Their Needs, Your Needs

1. Matthew 11:28
2. Matthew 7:9

Chapter 4: Delight

1. "Inheritance," written by Graham Cookie and Jonathan David Helser, © 2005 Bethel Music Publishing (ASCAP). All rights reserved. Used by permission.

2. Preston Britner et al., "Development and Preliminary Validation of the Caregiving Behavior System: Association with Child Attachment Classification in the Preschool Strange Situation," *Attachment & Human Development* 7, no. 1 (April 2005): 83–102, https://doi.org/10.1080/14616730500039861; Olrick, "Caregiving;" Kristin Bernard et al., "This Is My Baby: Foster Parents' Feelings of Commitment and Displays of Delight," *Infant Mental Health Journal* 32, no. 2 (March 2011): 251–262, https://doi.org/10.1002/imhj.20293; Ronald Rohner and Preston Britner, "Worldwide Mental Health Correlates of Parental Acceptance-Rejection: Review of Cross-Cultural and Intra-Cultural Evidence," *Cross-Cultural Research* 36, no. 1 (February 2002): 16–47, https://doi.org/10.1177/106939702129146316.

3. Sue Carter, "The Role of Oxytocin and Vasopressin in Attachment," *Psychodynamic Psychiatry* 45, no. 4 (December 2017): 499–517, https//doi.org:/10.1521/pdps.2017.45.4.499.

4. Ari Levine et al., "Oxytocin during Pregnancy and Early Postpartum: Individual Patterns and Maternal-Fetal Attachment," *Peptides* 28, no. 6

(June 2007): 1162–169, https://doi.org/10.1016/j/peptides.2007.04.016; Megan Galbally et al., "The Role of Oxytocin in Mother-Infant Relations: A Systematic Review of Human Studies," *Harvard Review of Psychiatry* 19, no. 1 (January 2011): 1–14, https://doi.org/10.3109 /10673229.2011.549771; Gregor Domes et al., "Oxytocin Improves 'Mind-Reading' in Humans," *Biological Psychiatry* 61, no. 6 (March 2007): 731–33, https://doi.org/10.1016/j.biopsych.2006.07.015; Anna MacKinnon et al., "Theory of Mind as a Link between Oxytocin and Maternal Behavior," *Psychoneuroendocrinology* 92 (June 2018): 87–94, https://doi.org/10.1016/j.psyneuen.2018.03.018.

5. Elizabeth Meins, "Sensitive Attunement to Infants' Internal States: Operationalizing the Construct of Mind-Mindedness," *Attachment & Human Development* 15, no. 5–6 (December 2013): 524–44, https://doi .org/10.1080/14616734.2013.830388.

6. Matthew 19:14

7. Matthew 3:17 ESV

Chapter 5: Support

1. Richard Ryan and Edward Deci, *Self-Determination Theory* (New York: Guilford, 2017).

2. Vansteenkiste et al., "On Psychological Growth."

3. Edward Deci et al., "Facilitating Optimal Motivation and Psychological Well-Being across Life's Domains," *Canadian Psychological Association* 49, no. 1 (2008): 14–23, https://doi.org/10.1037/0708-5591.49.1.14; Wendy Grolnick et al., "Parental Provision of Structure: Implementation and Correlates in Three Domains," *Merrill-Palmer Quarterly* 60, no. 3 (July 2014): 355–84, https://doi.org/10.1353/mpq.2014.0016.

4. L. S. Vygotsky, *Mind in Society: The Development of Higher Psychological Processes*, eds. Michael Cole, Vera John-Steiner, Sylvia Scribner, and Ellen Souberman (Cambridge, MA: Harvard University Press, 1978).

5. Kent Berridge et al., "Liking, Wanting and the Incentive-Sensitization Theory of Addiction," *The American Psychologist* 27, no. 8 (November 2016): 670–79, https//doi.org/10.1037/amp0000059; Oscar Arias-Carrion et al., "Dopamine, Learning, and Reward-Seeking Behavior," *Acta Neurobiologiae Experimentalis* 67, no. 4 (February 2007): 481–88.

6. Robert Sapolsky, *Behave: The Biology of Humans at Our Best and Worst* (New York: Penguin Random House, 2018), 70–74.

7. Richard Ryan et al., "Nature and Autonomy: An Organizational View of Social and Neurobiological Aspects of Self-Regulation in Behavior and Development," *Development and Psychopathology* 9 (February 1997):

701–28, https//doi.org/10.1017/S0954579497001405; Renee Landry et al., "Trust in Organismic Development, Autonomy Support, and Adaptation among Mothers and Their Children," *Motivation and Emotion* 32, no. 3 (September 2008): 173–88, https://doi.org/10.1007 /s11031-008-9092-2.

Chapter 6: Boundaries

1. Eddie Brummelman et al., "Origins of Narcissism in Children," *Proceedings of the National Academy of Sciences* 112, no. 12 (March 2015): 3659–662, https://doi.org/10.1073/pnas.1420870112.
2. Matthew 7:12
3. Cristina Colonnesi et al., "The Relation between Insecure Attachment and Child Anxiety: A Meta-Analytic Review," *Journal of Clinical Child and Adolescent Psychology* 40, no. 4 (July 2011): 630–45, https://doi.org /10.1080/15374416.2011.581623.
4. J. M. Fuster, "Prefrontal Cortex," in *International Encyclopedia of the Social and Behavioral Sciences Second Edition*, eds. Neil Smelser and Paul Baltes (Amsterdam: Elsevier, 2001), 11969–976, https://doi.org /10.1016/B0-08-043076-7/03465-3.
5. Allison Auchter et al., "Limbic System," in *International Encyclopedia of the Social and Behavioral Sciences Second Edition*, ed. James Wright (Amsterdam: Elsevier, 2015), 125–30, https://doi.org/10.1016 /B978-0-08-097086-8.55033-8.
6. Inga Schalinski et al., "Type and Timing of Adverse Childhood Experiences Differentially Affect Severity of PTSD, Dissociative and Depressive Symptoms in Adult Inpatients," *BMC Psychiatry*, 16:295 (August 2016), https://doi.org/10.1186/s12888-016-1004-5.
7. Rhoshel Lenroot et al., "Brain Development in Children and Adolescents: Insights from Anatomical Magnetic Resonance Imaging," *Neuroscience and Biobehavioral Reviews* 30, no. 6 (February 2006): 718–29, https://doi.org/10.1016/j.neubiorev.2006.06.001.
8. Sapolsky, *Behave*, 155.
9. Peter Fonagy and Elizabeth Allison, "What is Mentalization? The Concept and its Foundations in Developmental Research," in *Minding the Child: Mentalization-Based Interventions with Children, Young People, and Their Families*, eds. Nick Midgley and Ioanna Vrouva (New York: Rutledge, 2012), 11–34.
10. Daniel Siegel, *Mindsight: The New Science of Personal Transformation* (New York: Bantam, 2010).

Chapter 7: Protection

1. Gregory Boyle, *Tattoos on the Heart: The Power of Boundless Compassion* (New York: Free Press, 2010), 158.
2. "Children's Exposure to Violence," Childtrends, https://www .childtrends.org/indicators/childrens-exposure-to-violence.
3. "Children's Exposure to Violence, Crime, and Abuse: An Update," Office of Juvenile Justice and Delinquency Prevention, September 2015, https://www.ojjdp.gov/pubs/248547.pdf.
4. "About the CDC-Kaiser ACE Study," Centers for Disease Control and Prevention, https://www.cdc.gov/violenceprevention /childabuseandneglect/acestudy/about.html.
5. Felitti, "Relationship of Childhood Abuse," 245–58.
6. "The Truth About ACES," Robert Wood Johnson Foundation, May 12, 2013, https://www.rwjf.org/en/library/infographics/the-truth -about-aces.html.
7. Helen MacDonald et al., "Longitudinal Association between Infant Disorganized Attachment and Childhood Posttraumatic Stress Symptoms," *Development and Psychopathology* 20, no. 2 (Fall 2008): 493–508, https://doi.org/10.1017/S0954579408000242; Christin Ogle et al., "The Relation between Insecure Attachment and Posttraumatic Stress: Early Life versus Adulthood Traumas," *Psychological Trauma: Theory, Research, Practice and Policy* 7, no. 4 (2015): 324–32, https:// doi.org/10.1037/tra0000015; Karlen Lyons-Ruth et al., "From Infant Attachment Disorganization to Adult Dissociation: Relational Adaptations of Traumatic Experiences?," *The Psychiatric Clinics of North America* 29, no. 1 (March 2006): 63–86, https://doi.org/10.1016/j.psc .2005.10.011.
8. Robert Plomin et al., "Common Disorders Are Quantitative Traits," *Nature Review Genetics* 10, no. 12 (October 2009): 872–78, https://doi .org/10.1038/nrg2670.
9. Robert Anda, et al., "The Enduring Effects of Abuse and Related Adverse Experiences in Childhood: A Convergence of Evidence from Neurobiology and Epidemiology," *European Archives of Psychiatry and Clinical Neuroscience* 256, no. 3 (April 2006): 174–86, https://doi .org/10.1007/s00406-005-0624-4. Schalinski, "Type and Timing."
10. DeKlyen, "Attachment and Psychopathology." Michelle Enlow et al., "Mother-Infant Attachment and the Intergenerational Transmission of Posttraumatic Stress Disorder," *Development and Psychopathology* 26, no. 1 (February 2014): 41–65, https://doi.org/10.1017 /S0954579413000515; Lauren Sippel et al., "Oxytocin Receptor

Gene Polymorphisms, Attachment, and PTSD: Results from the National Health and Resilience in Veterans Study," *Journal of Psychiatric Research* 94 (November 2017): 139–47, https://doi.org/10.1016/j.jpsychires.2017.07.008; Sarit Guttmann-Steinmetz et al., "Attachment and Externalizing Disorders: A Developmental Psychopathology Perspective," *Journal of the American Academy of Child and Adolescent Psychiatry* 45, no. 4 (April 2006): 440–51, https://doi.org/10.1097/01.chi.0000196422.42599.63.

11. Jean Twenge, *iGen: Why Today's Super-Connected Kids Are Growing Up Less Rebellious, More Tolerant, Less Happy—and Completely Unprepared for Adulthood (and What That Means for the Rest of Us)* (New York: Atria, 2017); Benoit Denizet-Lewis, "Why Are More American Teenagers Than Ever Suffering from Severe Anxiety?" *The New York Times Magazine*, October 11, 2017, https://www.nytimes.com/2017/10/11/magazine/why-are-more-american-teenagers-than-ever-suffering-from-severe-anxiety.html?module=inline. A comprehensive review of the ACE study findings can be found at https://www.cdc.gov/violenceprevention/acestudy/about.html, along with extensive resources for reducing child maltreatment in your community. For additional resources for child trauma, visit https://www.nctsn.org/.

12. John 16:33

13. John 17:15, 18

Chapter 8: Comfort

1. Julia McQuade et al., "Parent Emotion Socialization and Preadolescent's Social and Emotional Adjustment: Moderating Effects of Autonomic Nervous System Reactivity," *Biological Psychology* 130 (December 2017): 67–76, https://doi.org/10.1016/j.biopsycho.2017.10.007; Elizabeth Shewark et al., "Mothers' and Fathers' Emotion Socialization and Children's Emotion Regulation: A Within-Family Model," *British Journal of Social Psychology* 24, no. 2 (May 2015): 266–84, https://doi.org/10.1111/sode.12095; Danli Li et al., "Intergenerational Transmission of Emotion Regulation through Parents' Reactions to Children's Negative Emotions: Tests of Unique, Actor, Partner, and Mediating Effects," *Children and Youth Services Review* 101 (June 2019): 113–22, https://doi.org/10.1016/j.childyouth.2019.03.038; Rachel Miller-Slough et al., "Maternal and Paternal Reactions to Child Sadness Predict Children's Psychosocial Outcomes: A Family-Centered Approach," *Social Development* 27, no. 3 (August 2018): 495–509, https://doi.org/10.1111/sode.12244. John Gottman et al., "Parental Meta-Emotion Philosophy

and the Emotional Life of Families: Theoretical Models and Preliminary Data," *Journal of Family Psychology*, 10, no. 3 (September 1996): 243–68, https://doi.org/10.1037/0893-3200.10.3.243.

2. Sroufe et al., *The Development of the Person*, 154–6, 180–1, 205.
3. Leslie Brody and Judith Hall, "Gender and Emotion in Context," in *Handbook of Emotions Third Edition*, eds. Michael Lewis, Jeannette Haviland-Jones, and Lisa Barrett (New York: Guilford, 2008), 395–408; Tara Chaplin, "Gender and Emotion Expression: A Developmental Contextual Perspective," *Emotion Review: Journal of the International Society for Research on Emotion* 7, no. 1 (January 2015): 14–21, https://doi.org/10.1177/1754073914544408; Tara Chaplin et al., "Parental Socialization of Emotion Expression: Gender Differences and Relations to Child Adjustment," *Emotion* 5, no.1 (April 2005): 80–88, https://doi.org/10.1037/1528–3542.5.1.80; Andrew Reiner, "Talking to Boys the Way We Talk to Girls," *New York Times*, June 15, 2017, https://www.nytimes.com/2017/06/15/well/family/talking-to-boys-the-way-we-talk-to-girls.html; "The State of Gender Equality for U.S. Adolescents." Plan International USA, https://www.planusa.org/docs/state-of-gender-equality-2018.pdf.
4. John 11:4
5. John 11:43

Chapter 9: Equipping

1. Anthony Mulac et al., "Male/Female Gaze in Same-Sex and Mixed-Sex Dyads: Gender-Linked Differences and Mutual Influence," *Human Communication Research* 13, no. 3 (March 1987): 323–43, https://doi.org/10.1111/j.1468-2958.1987.tb00108.x.
2. Sherry Turkle, "The Flight From Conversation," *New York Times*, October 25, 2012, https://www.nytimes.com/2012/04/22/opinion/sunday/the-flight-from-conversation.html.
3. Jean Twenge, "Have Smartphones Destroyed a Generation?," *The Atlantic*, August 3, 2017, http://theatlantic.com/magazine/archive/2017/09/has-the-smartphone-destroyed-a-generation/534198/.
4. Ross Thompson et al., "Early Understandings of Emotion, Morality, and Self: Developing a Working Model," *Advances in Child Development and Behavior* 31 (February 2003): 137–71, https://doi.org/10.1016/S0065-2407(03)31004-3.
5. Janine Oostenbroek et al., "The Emergence of Forgiveness in Young Children," *Child Development* (online April 2018), https://doi.org/10.1111/cdev.13069.

6. Matthew 7:24–25
7. Matthew 7:15
8. Matthew 7:16

Chapter 10: A Sustainable Path of Connection

1. "Compulsory Classes Will Help Right the Wrong after Te Reo Māori 'Beaten' Out of School Children a Generation ago—Sir Pita Sharples," 1newsnow. https://www.tvnz.co.nz/one-news/new-zealand /compulsory-classes-help-right-wrong-after-te-reo-m-ori-beaten -school-children-generation-ago-sir-pita-sharples.
2. "History of the Māori Language," New Zealand Ministry for Culture and Heritage, https://nzhistory.govt.nz/culture/maori -language-week/history-of-the-maori-language.
3. Link, "Tuhia" Track 2 on Kia Kaha, 2017.
4. D. W. Winnicott, *The Maturational Processes and the Facilitating Environment: Studies in the Theory of Emotional Development* (London: Hogarth, 1965).
5. Mario Mikulincer and Phillip Shaver, "Adult Attachment and Emotion Regulation," in *Handbook of Attachment, Third Edition: Theory, Research, and Clinical Applications*, eds. Jude Cassidy and Phillip Shaver (New York: Guilford, 2016): 507–33.
6. Maria Brambilla et al., "Autonomous versus Controlled Religiosity: Family and Group Antecedents," *The International Journal for the Psychology of Religion* 25, no. 3 (February 2015): 193–210, https://doi .org/10.1080/10508619.2014.888902; Tim Kasser et al., "Early Family Experiences and Adult Values: A 26-Year, Prospective Longitudinal Study," *Personality and Social Psychology Bulletin* 28, no. 6 (June 2002): 826–35, https://doi.org/10.1177/0146167202289011.
7. Matthew 12:34
8. John 18:10; Matthew 16:22; Matthew 26:33
9. Matthew 16:18
10. Matthew 26:72
11. Matthew 26:75
12. John 21:15
13. John 21:16